*QUANTITATIVE SYSTEMS
for BUSINESS*

QSB

QUANTITATIVE SYSTEMS for BUSINESS
QSB

YIH-LONG CHANG
The Ohio State University

ROBERT S. SULLIVAN
The University of Texas

PRENTICE-HALL, Englewood Cliffs, New Jersey 07632

Library of Congress Cataloging-in-Publication Data

Chang, Yih-Long.
   Quantitative systems for business.

   1. Management science. I. Sullivan, Robert S.
II. Title.
T56.C427 1986   658   85-31180
ISBN 0-13-747007-X
ISBN 0-13-747015-0 (disc)

Editorial/production supervision: Susan Fisher
Cover design: Lundgren Graphics, Ltd.
Manufacturing buyers: Ed O'Dougherty and Ron Chapman

© 1986 by Prentice-Hall
A Division of Simon & Schuster, Inc.
Englewood Cliffs, New Jersey 07632

All rights reserved. No part of this book may be
reproduced, in any form or by any means,
without permission in writing from the publisher.

Printed in the United States of America

10 9 8 7 6 5 4 3 2 1

ISBN 0-13-747007-X   {BK}   01
ISBN 0-13-747015-0   {BK/DISK} 01

Prentice-Hall International (UK) Limited, *London*
Prentice-Hall of Australia Pty. Limited, *Sydney*
Prentice-Hall Canada Inc., *Toronto*
Prentice-Hall Hispanoamericana, S.A., *Mexico*
Prentice-Hall of India Private Limited, *New Delhi*
Prentice-Hall of Japan, Inc., *Tokyo*
Prentice-Hall of Southeast Asia Pte. Ltd., *Singapore*
Editora Prentice-Hall do Brasil, Ltda., *Rio de Janeiro*
Whitehall Books Limited, *Wellington, New Zealand*

Contents

Preface .... *ix*

Quick and Dirty Procedure for Getting QSB Started .... *xi*

Chapter 1—Introduction to QSB *1*
    Special Features 1
    Contents of QSB 1
    QSB in Instruction and Learning 3
    QSB in Decision Making 3
    Organization of This Manual 4

Chapter 2—Getting Started with QSB *5*
    Required Equipment 5
    IBM PC Keyboard—Some Conventions in the Use of QSB 5
    Getting Your QSB Diskette Ready to Use 6
    Formatting a Data Diskette 6
    QSB(I) and QSB(II) 7
    Getting Started with QSB 8
    When Things Go Wrong and Error Messages 8

Chapter 3—A Tutorial Guide to QSB *10*
    Problem Solving with QSB 10
    Menu Structure 11
    A Tutorial Example 12

Chapter 4—Linear Programming (LP) *22*
    Overview of the LP Decision Support System 22
    Special Notes on the LP Program 22
    Solving Problems with LP 23
    Example 24
    The Big M Method—an Example 29
    Exercises 31

Chapter 5—Integer Linear Programming (ILP) *34*
    Overview of the ILP Decision Support System 34
    Special Notes on the ILP Program 34
    Solving Problems with ILP 35
    Example 36
    0-1 Integer Linear Programming Problem 41
    Exercises 42

Chapter 6—Transportation Problems (TRP)   *46*
    Overview of the TRP Decision Support System   46
    Special Notes on the TRP Program   46
    Solving Problems with TRP   47
    Example   48
    Finding an Initial Solution—Vogel's Approximation Method (VAM)   53
    Exercises   54

Chapter 7—Assignment Problems (ASMP)   *57*
    Overview of the ASMP Decision Support System   57
    Special Notes on the ASMP Program   57
    Solving Problems with ASMP   58
    Example   58
    Exercises   63

Chapter 8—Network Modeling (NET)   *66*
    Overview of the NET Decision Support System   66
    Special Notes on the NET Program   66
    Solving Problems with NET   67
    Examples   68
    The Shortest Route Problem   68
    A Minimal Spanning Tree   72
    The Maximal Flow Problem   73
    Exercises   76

Chapter 9—Critical Path Method (CPM)   *78*
    Overview of the CPM Decision Support System   78
    Special Notes on the CPM Program   78
    Solving Problems with CPM   79
    Example   80
    Exercises   85

Chapter 10—Program Evaluation and Review Technique (PERT)   *88*
    Overview of the PERT Decision Support System   88
    Special Notes on the PERT Program   88
    Solving Problems with PERT   89
    Example   90
    Exercises   94

Chapter 11—Dynamic Programming (DP)   *98*
    Overview of the DP Decision Support System   98
    Special Notes on the DP Program   98
    Solving Problems with DP   99
    Examples   99
    Stagecoach Problem   100

Knapsack Problem　105
　　　Production and Inventory Control Problem　108
　　　Exercises　111

Chapter 12—Inventory Theory (INVT) — 113
　　　Overview of the INVT Decision Support System　113
　　　Special Notes on the INVT Program　113
　　　Solving Problems with INVT　113
　　　Examples　114
　　　Economic Order Quantity　114
　　　Price Discounts　118
　　　Exercises　119

Chapter 13—Queuing Theory (QUEUE) — 121
　　　Overview of the QUEUE Decision Support System　121
　　　Special Notes on the QUEUE Program　121
　　　Solving Problems with QUEUE　121
　　　Examples　122
　　　M/M/1 System　122
　　　M/M/2 System　125
　　　Exercises　126

Chapter 14—Queuing System Simulation (QSIM) — 129
　　　Overview of the QSIM Decision Support System　129
　　　Special Notes on the QSIM Program　129
　　　Solving Problems with QSIM　130
　　　Example　131
　　　Simulating the Second Configuration　138
　　　Exercises　139

Chapter 15—Decision and Probability Theory (DSPB) — 141
　　　Overview of the DSPB Decision Support System　141
　　　Special Notes on the DSPB Program　141
　　　Solving Problems with DSPB　142
　　　Examples　142
　　　Mean and Variance　143
　　　Bayesian Analysis　146
　　　Payoff Table Analysis　146
　　　A Decision Tree　151
　　　Exercises　153

Chapter 16—Markov Process (MKV) — 158
　　　Overview of the MKV Decision Support System　158
　　　Special Notes on the MKV Program　158
　　　Solving Problems with MKV　158

>   Example   159
>   Exercises   164

Chapter 17—Time Series Forecasting (TSFC) — *166*
>   Overview of the TSFC Decision Support System   166
>   Special Notes on the TSFC Program   166
>   Solving Problems with TSFC   166
>   Example   167
>   Exercises   171

Appendix — *173*

PREFACE

QSB (Quantitative Systems for Business) is a software package that contains the most popular problem-solving algorithms in the management sciences. Topics covered in QSB are as follows:

1. Linear programming (LP)
2. Integer linear programming (ILP)
3. Transportation problems
4. Assignment problems
5. Network modeling
6. Critical path method (CPM)
7. Program Evaluation and Review Technique (PERT)
8. Dynamic programming
9. Inventory theory
10. Queuing theory
11. Queuing system simulation
12. Decision and probability theory
13. Markov process
14. Time series forecasting

QSB can help the instructor explain how a scientific algorithm works. The students will find that learning the management sciences through the use of QSB is interesting and less intimidating. QSB also demonstrates the power of the microcomputer in problem solving. Furthermore, a practitioner might use QSB in the decision process. Because of the friendliness of this microcomputer software, the user will not feel the difficulty of the mainframe.

The manual is a valuable addition to the use of QSB. Although QSB itself is very friendly, the manual contains the detailed steps on how to use QSB. Some of the special features, such as the LP program's ability to read the files saved in the ILP program, are also described in the manual.

Chapter 1 introduces the contents and capabilities of QSB. Chapter 2 describes the steps for getting started. When you receive your QSB diskettes, you should follow the steps in Chapter 2 to make them ready. For a first-time user, Chapter 3 presents a tutorial on how to use QSB. This tutorial guide could be generalized in all QSB programs. Chapters 4 to 17 correspond to programs 1 to E in QSB. Each chapter describes the steps in using a specific program. Some exercise problems are included in Chapters 4 to 17 so that you can practice. Selected problem solutions are listed in the appendix.

Quick and Dirty Procedure for Getting QSB Started

1. **Copy DOS to QSB** — follow these steps to copy the operating system onto the QSB diskettes.
   (1) Insert the system diskette (DOS 2.0 or equivalent, which is usually provided with your PC) into the A (left) diskette drive.
   (2) If the power is off, turn the power on and proceed to step (4).
   (3) If the power is already on, reset the PC by pressing the "Ctrl", "Alt", and "Del" keys simultaneously.
   (4) Wait a few seconds and then follow the instructions presented on the screen either to enter the date and time or press the ENTER key.
   (5) Now the screen displays the following prompt:
   A⟩
   (6) Insert your diskette labeled (QSB(I) into the B (right) diskette drive. Type the following and then press the ENTER key:
   A⟩B:STARTUP
   (7) The diskette drives will whirl for a short time as the operating system is copied onto QSB (I). When the drive stops, repeat from step (5) for QSB(II). Then do the next step to specify the type of printer you will use.

2. **Specify the Type of Printer** — follow these steps to specify the type of printer you will use.
   (1) Insert the QSB(I) diskette into the A (left) diskette drive.
   (2) Type the following and then press the ENTER key:
   A⟩QSB
   (3) Wait a few seconds, the QSB logo will be presented on the screen. By hitting any key, the permission message will be displayed. By hitting any key again, the program menu will be displayed.
   (4) Choose option F from the program menu to specify the type of printer you will use. Enter "0" if you wish to use IBM PC Graphics Printer or Compatibles; otherwise enter "1".
   (5) Remove QSB(I) and insert QSB(II), then repeat step (4) for QSB(II).

Then, you may use a write protect tab to cover the notch to protect the diskette.

Chapter 1
INTRODUCTION TO QSB

QSB (Quantitative Systems for Business) is an interactive, user-friendly decision support system that covers most topics taught in introductory courses in management science. The primary purpose of QSB is to assist the instructor in teaching these topics. By letting students gain hands-on experience in problem-solving, QSB makes these topics less intimidating. However, QSB also has the capacity to assist practitioners in addressing problems of moderate size. In the following sections, the special features of QSB are discussed.

Special Features

User-friendly: QSB is specially designed for those who have no experience in solving quantitative business problems on a personal computer, as well as for those who are familiar with personal computers but do not want to do any computer programming. The information and messages presented in QSB are easily understandable. For the decision maker, QSB displays brief solutions to the problems; for management scientists and students, QSB can display detailed and understandable intermediate steps in the solution of the problems.

Menu-driven: QSB uses a menu-driven structure that enables users to recognize the options available to address a problem. The highest level menu is the program menu. Once a program is selected, the associated function menu appears. This enables the user to enter a new problem, read an existing problem, and so on. Several options also have associated menus to direct the user.

Easy data entry and modification: QSB enables users to enter data from the keyboard or read data from a disk(ette) if the data have been stored. Entry formats are designed to be compatible with most conventional textbook formats. Therefore, users who have studied the basic concepts of management science will find that problem structuring and data entry are easy with QSB. Every program has the capacity to modify an existing problem.

Contents of QSB

QSB covers most of the popular topics in management science. Table 1.1 provides an overview of the topics and programs covered by QSB and presented in more detail in this text.

CHAPTER 1

Table 1.1. Contents of QSB

No.	Topic	Capabilities
1.	Linear programming	Uses the revised simplex method with up to 40 variables and 40 constraints.
2.	Integer linear programming	Uses the branch and bound method with up to 20 variables and 20 constraints.
3.	Transportation problems	Uses the modified distribution method with up to 50 sources and 50 destinations.
4.	Assignment problems	Uses the Hungarian method with up to 60 objects and 60 tasks.
5.	Network modeling	The shortest route, minimal spanning tree and maximal flow problems.
6.	Project scheduling—CPM	Critical path method with up to 200 activities and crashing analysis.
7.	Project scheduling—PERT	Program evaluation and review technique with up to 200 activities.
8.	Dynamic programming	The stagecoach, knapsack, and production and inventory control problems.
9.	Inventory theory	EOQ, EOQ with discount, and newsboy problems.
10.	Queuing theory	M/M/1, M/M/1 with finite queue, M/M/1 with finite source, M/M/c, M/M/c with finite source, and more.
11.	Queuing system simulation	Single-stage queuing system with up to 20 servers and 20 queues.
12.	Decision theory	Mean and variance analysis, Bayesian analysis, payoff analysis, and decision tree.
13.	Markov process	Allows for 50 states of the system.
14.	Time series forecasting	Moving average, exponential smoothing, linear regression, and more.

QSB in Instruction and Learning

Most of the programs in QSB have an optional ability to display detailed solution procedures. This option can help both instructors and students by making algorithms easier to explain and understand. For example, when using the simplex method to solve the following linear programming model, the LP program can display every simplex tableau with the highlighted entering and leaving variables. For more information, see Chapters 3 and 4.

Maximize $\quad 4 X1 + 6 X2 + 3 X3 + 1 X4$
Subject to: $\quad 1.5 X1 + 2 X2 + 4 X3 + 3 X4 \leq 550$
$\qquad\qquad\;\; 4 X1 + 1 X2 + 2 X3 + 1 X4 \leq 700$
$\qquad\qquad\;\; 2 X1 + 3 X2 + 1 X3 + 2 X4 \leq 300$
$\qquad\qquad\qquad\qquad\qquad\quad$ any $Xn \geq 0$

QSB in Decision Making

Management science is widely used in business decision making. To illustrate a typical application, consider the following example. ABC Oil Company has three oil storage depots and four demand points for oil. Management wants a shipping schedule that minimizes the total transportation cost and that does not exceed storage capacities. Assume that capacities and cost information are given as shown in Table 1.2. The modified distribution method (transportation simplex) is usually used to solve this type of problem. By using the QSB Transportation Program, management can determine the optimal shipping schedule very quickly. Table 1.3 displays the solution for the ABC shipping problem.

Table 1.2. Capacities and unit costs for ABC Company

		Dallas	Kansas	Tampa	Miami	Supply capacity
Storage	Boston	5	4	5	6	100
	Denver	3	3	6	6	200
	Austin	2	5	7	8	400
	Demand	200	100	150	250	

(Demand point columns: Dallas, Kansas, Tampa, Miami)

CHAPTER 1

Table 1.3.

Summary of Results for ABC						Page : 1	
From	To	Shipment	Unit cost	From	To	Shipment	Unit cost
Boston	Dallas	0.0	5.000	Denver	Tampa	0.0	6.000
Boston	Kansas	0.0	4.000	Denver	Miami	100.0	6.000
Boston	Tampa	100.0	5.000	Austin	Dallas	200.0	2.000
Boston	Miami	0.0	6.000	Austin	Kansas	0.0	5.000
Denver	Dallas	0.0	3.000	Austin	Tampa	50.0	7.000
Denver	Kansas	100.0	3.000	Austin	Miami	150.0	8.000
Minimum value of OBJ = 3350 (multiple sols.) Iterations = 3							

Organization of This Manual

Chapter 1:   Introduction to QSB

Chapter 2:   Getting Started with QSB
This chapter describes everything you need to do and to know before using QSB. Some common errors and messages are discussed.

Chapter 3:   A Tutorial Guide to QSB
A general quantitative business problem-solving procedure using QSB is provided. The detailed steps to use QSB are illustrated. A new user will find this chapter interesting and useful.

Chapters 4 to 17:   How to Use Each Program
Each chapter describes one of the 14 programs that solve special types of quantitative business problems. A standard procedure for using these programs is established and demonstrated. These chapters are written independently so that you can use each program individually.

Chapter 2
GETTING STARTED WITH QSB

This chapter covers the conventions and procedures used with QSB. If you are a first-time user of QSB, this chapter will give you all the background information you need to get started.

Required Equipment

QSB is designed to run on the IBM personal computer or an IBM PC compatible computer. The following are the minimum hardware and software requirements for QSB:

Required: IBM PC with at least 64K memory; at least one disk(ette) drive; DOS 2.0 version

Optional: A second disk(ette) drive to facilitate storing and retrieving data; a printer

IBM PC Keyboard—Some Conventions in the Use of QSB

If you are familiar with the IBM PC, you may choose to skip this section. Table 2.1 lists some keys that you will use with QSB.

Table 2.1. Important keys in QSB

Key	When to use
A–Z, a–z	Define problem names and variable names
0-9, "."	Data entry and option selection
Esc, "/"	Special control when in data entry mode
ENTER (↵)	Data entry (after you type one data item)
BACKSPACE (←)	Data entry (if you want to move the cursor back)
SPACE BAR	Data entry
Arrow keys (↓,↑,→,←)	For selecting a menu item or function
F8	Press this key for copying the screen to the printer
F9	Return to the program menu

CHAPTER 2

Table 2.1. *(Cont.)* Important keys in QSB

Key	When to use
F10	Exit from QSB.
Ctrl, Alt, and Del	Press these keys simultaneously for reloading (reactivating) QSB
Screen contrast knob	Appropriate adjustment will highlight the output

Getting Your QSB Diskette Ready to Use

If your QSB diskettes are new and have not been used before, follow these steps to copy the operating system onto the QSB diskettes.

1. Insert the system diskette (DOS 2.0 or equivalent, which is usually provided with your PC) into the A (left) diskette drive.

2. If the power is off, turn the power on and proceed to step 4.

3. If the power is already on, reset the PC by pressing the "Ctrl," "Alt," and "Del" keys simultaneously.

4. Wait a few seconds and then follow the instructions presented on the screen either to enter the date and time or press the ENTER key.

5. Now the screen displays the following prompt:

    A>

6. Insert your diskette labeled QSB(I) into the B (right) diskette drive. Type the following and then press the ENTER key:

    A>B:STARTUP

7. The diskette drives will whirl for a short time as the operating system is copied onto QSB(I). When the drive stops, return to step 5 and use diskette labeled QSB(II).

Formatting a Data Diskette

You should save problems on diskettes separate from QSB(I) and QSB(II). A separate data diskette will have to be formatted in order to be used with your IBM PC. The following steps will format a diskette. Note that when you format a diskette, old data are lost.

1. Insert the system diskette (DOS 2.0 or equivalent) into the A (left) diskette drive.

2. If the power is off, turn the power on and proceed to step 4.

3. If the power is already on, reset the PC by pressing the "Ctrl," "Alt," and "Del" keys simultaneously.

4. Wait a few seconds and then follow the instructions presented on the screen either to enter the date and time or press the ENTER key.

5. Now the screen displays

    A>

6. Insert your blank diskette into the B (right) diskette drive. Type the following and then press the ENTER key:

    A>FORMAT B:

7. After a few seconds, you will be asked if you want to format another diskette. If you do not, answer "N." The prompt A> will be displayed again. If you do, answer "Y" and follow the directions on the display. You are now ready to use QSB.

QSB(I) and QSB(II)

QSB(I) and QSB(II) contain programs to address common types of quantitative business problems. Following are some examples:

QSB(I):
1. Linear programming (LP)
2. Integer linear programming (ILP)
3. Transportation problem (TRP)
4. Assignment problem (ASMP)
5. Network modeling (NET)
6. Project scheduling—CPM (CPM)
7. Project scheduling—PERT (PERT)

QSB(II):
8. Dynamic programming (DP)
9. Inventory theory (INVT)
10. Queuing theory (QUEUE)
11. Queuing system simulation (QSIM)
12. Decision and probability theory (DSPB)
13. Markov process (MKV)
14. Time series forecasting (TSFC)

CHAPTER 2

Two extra files—PTR.QSB and FNMENU.QSB—are included in each diskette for implementing QSB. QSB(I) and QSB(II) also contain sample problem files for each program: LPTEST, ILPTEST, TRPTEST, and so on. Each of these programs is described in detail in subsequent chapters.

Getting Started with QSB

You are now ready to use QSB. The following procedure will load a QSB diskette.

1. Insert the appropriate QSB diskette (I or II depending on the program desired) into the A (left) diskette drive.

2. If the power is off, turn the power on and proceed to step 4.

3. If the power is already on, reset the PC by pressing the "Ctrl," "Alt," and "Del" keys simultaneously.

4. Wait a few seconds and then follow the instructions presented on the screen either to enter the date and time or press the ENTER key. QSB will then automatically load itself.

5. Now simply follow the instruction shown on the screen. You will see the program menu from which you may select an option.

If you use QSB first time, choose Option "F" from the program menu to specify the type of printer you will use.

When Things Go Wrong and Error Messages

Nothing is perfect. Table 2.2 shows the most likely problems you may have and the procedures to correct them. However, a good rule is to save your problem data to avoid losing them in case of hardware or software problems.

Table 2.2. Problem and error corrections

Problem or message	Correction
This program is not on this diskette	Change QSB diskette.
You select a wrong program	Use option 9 in the function menu to return to the program menu.
You select incorrect function option	Press the ENTER key again to return to the function menu.

Table 2.2. *(Cont.)* Problem and error corrections

Problem or message	Correction
You find a previous data entry to be incorrect during data entry	Use BACKSPACE key to go back to the previous position and correct it.
You move to a wrong page during data entry	Use the "Esc" or "/" key to change page.
Printer not ready	Check printer or press the "Esc" key to return to the function menu.
Disk not ready	Check disk drive or press the "Esc" key to return to the function menu.
Disk full	Change diskette or press the "Esc" key to return to the function menu.
File not found	Check file name or press the "Esc" key to return to the function menu.
Bad file name	Use legal file name or press "Esc" key to return to the function menu.
Error xx on line xxxx	Press the "Esc" key to return to the function menu.
Other problems	Press "Ctrl," "Alt," and "Del" keys simultaneously to reload QSB. Note that this load action will destroy data if your problem has not been saved on a data diskette.

Chapter 3
A TUTORIAL GUIDE TO QSB

This chapter details the steps necessary to use QSB in problem-solving. First, a general problem-solving procedure using QSB is presented, and a tree structure of menus is described. A step-by-step procedure is then demonstrated by solving a linear programming example. This can be generalized to other programs in QSB.

Problem Solving with QSB

Figure 3.1 shows the general problem-solving structure of QSB. The procedure is described as follows:

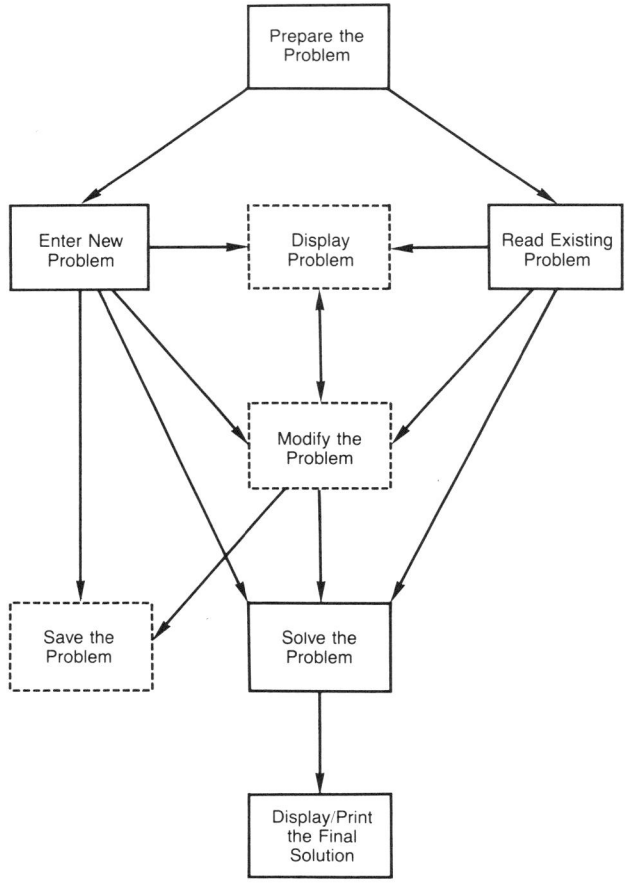

FIGURE 3.1. Problem solving with QSB.

Step 1. Prepare the problem: Analyze and formulate your problem.

Step 2. Enter or read a problem: You can use option 2 of the function menu to enter a new problem, or you can use option 3 of the function menu to read a previously saved problem from a data disk(ette).

Step 3. Display and/or print input data (optional): You may display and/or print the problem that has been entered in step 2. This display can help you verify that your problem data are entered correctly.

Step 4. Modify problem (optional): By using option 7 of the function menu, you may perform several kinds of modifications, such as changing the number of variables and changing the number of constraints on your problem when necessary.

Step 5. Solve problem: Option 5 of the function menu allows you to display intermediate solution steps, such as the simplex tableau of linear programming, as well as the final solution.

Step 6. Display and/or print final solution: After the problem has been solved, option 8 of the function menu will display and/or print the final solution.

Step 7. Save a problem: If you want to keep your problem on a disk(ette), use option 6 of the function menu. This step can be performed any time after the problem has been entered.

Menu Structure

QSB incorporates the advantages of a menu-driven structure so that users can follow the instructions on the screen without memorizing command names. This makes QSB very easy and friendly to use. Figure 3.2 shows the tree structure of the QSB menus. The first level of menus is the program menu from which the user can choose a specific program for problem solving. After a program is selected, a general function menu, which is typically composed of ten functional capabilities, will be displayed. The user may then select a specific function, and a submenu for advanced operations will be displayed.

CHAPTER 3

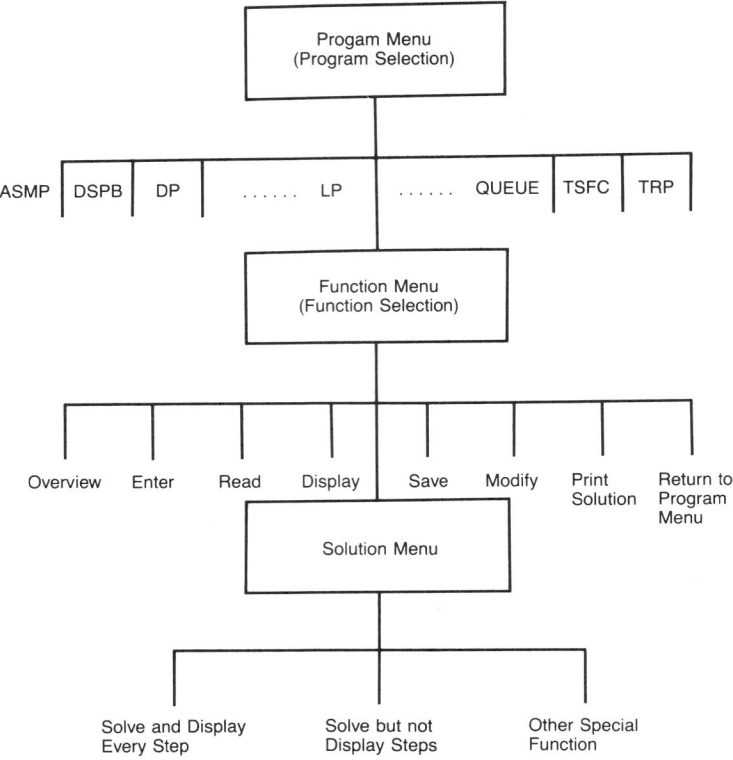

FIGURE 3.2. Tree structure of QSB.

A Tutorial Example

In this section we assume you have already prepared QSB(I) and QSB(II) by using the procedure "Getting Your QSB Diskette Ready to Use" described in Chapter 2. The steps in the following example can be generalized to each program module. A new user will find these steps simple and useful. However, you may refer to a specific chapter (4 to 17) when you solve a particular type of problem.

Example Problem: You are asked to solve the following LP problem:

$$\text{Maximize} \quad 4A + 6B + 3C + 1D$$
$$\text{Subject to:} \quad 1.5A + 2B + 4C + 3D \leq 550$$
$$4A + 1B + 2C + 1D \leq 700$$
$$2A + 3B + 1C + 2D \leq 300$$
$$A, B, C, D \geq 0$$

The following steps demonstrate a typical detailed procedure for using QSB:

A Tutorial Guide to QSB

Step 1. Start up QSB:

1.1. Follow the steps of "Getting Started with QSB" outlined in Chapter 2 to load the QSB program. You will be asked to enter current date and time. If you don't want to, just press the ENTER key.

1.2. The QSB logo will be shown on the screen. Hit any key, and the program menu will be displayed, as shown in Fig. 3.3.

```
              Welcome to QSB (Quantitative Systems for Business)!
You may choose from following management science decision support systems:

Code                               Code
No.       Program                  No.       Program

1 -- Linear programming            9 -- Inventory theory
2 -- Integer linear programming    A -- Queuing theory
3 -- Transportation problem        B -- Queuing system simulation
4 -- Assignment problem            C -- Decision/probability theory
5 -- Network modeling              D -- Markov process
6 -- Project scheduling -- CPM     E -- Time series forecasting
7 -- Project scheduling -- PERT    F -- Specify the type of printer
8 -- Dynamic programming           G -- Exit from QSB
```

        ** QSB(I): Programs 1 to 7, QSB(II): Programs 8 to E **

FIGURE 3.3. Program menu.

Step 2. Select a program: Now you have the program menu. Options 1 to 9 and A to E represent different programs you may choose. If your printer is not a dot-matrix printer, you may use option F to specify it. This will make the solution outputs less confusing. If you don't want to go to any program, option G will let you exit from QSB. You can make a selection in two ways. One is to hit any one of the "1" to "9" and "A" to "G" keys, and QSB will directly load the selected program. The other method is to use the arrow keys (the up and down, left and right keys) to move the inverse-video image to the desired option; then hit the ENTER key. QSB will load the selected program. If the blinking message "This program is not on this diskette." is shown at the bottom of the screen, you are using the wrong diskette. Change to another QSB diskette and hit the ENTER key; the desired program will then be loaded.

2.1. The example is an LP problem. Choose option 1 from the program menu, and the blinking message "Loading program, please standby." will be displayed.

2.2. After a few seconds, the LP program will be loaded, and the function menu will be displayed on the screen, as shown in Fig. 3.4.

CHAPTER 3

```
Welcome to your Linear Programming (LP) Decision Support System!
         The options available for LP are as follows.
 If you are a first-time user, you might benefit from option 1.

    Option              Function

       1       ----   Overview of LP Decision Support System
       2       ----   Enter new problem
       3       ----   Read existing problem from disk(ette)
       4       ----   Display and/or print input data
       5       ----   Solve problem
       6       ----   Save problem on disk(ette)
       7       ----   Modify problem
       8       ----   Display and/or print final solution
       9       ----   Return to the program menu
       0       ----   Exit from QSB
```

FIGURE 3.4. Function menu of the LP program.

Choosing an option from the function menu is similar to choosing an option from the program menu. By using the numeric keys or the combination of the arrow keys and the ENTER key, you can select each functional option. Here are the descriptions of these functional options:

Option 1: You can see the overview of a specific program. It tells you the capabilities and restrictions of that program.

Option 2: By selecting this option, you can enter a new problem into the program. This is the way to start with a program when you have a new problem.

Option 3: You may read a previously saved problem by using this option. This will be described in more detail later.

Option 4: After you have entered a problem or read a saved problem, you may use this option to display and/or print the problem.

Option 5: This is the option to solve your problem. It provides you with several suboptions to facilitate your solution process. Also, the function to display and/or print the final solution will automatically follow.

Option 6: Use this option to save an entered problem on a desired disk(ette).

Option 7: This option allows you to change most of the problem structure. It will save a lot of time when you have only a few revisions.

Option 8: Most programs in QSB have this option to display and/or print the final solution.

Option 9:   QSB will go back to the program menu if you choose this option.

Option 10:   Exit from QSB.

You should begin with option 1 (overview) when you are using a program for the first time. If you choose options 4 to 8 before you use option 2 or 3 to enter or read a problem, the program will give a blinking warning message. (Try option 5 to see what happens!) If that happens, press any key, and the function menu will return.

Step 3.   <u>Enter a problem</u>: Now you have the function menu on the screen and an LP problem to solve. By selecting option 2 (press the "2" key or use the "down" key to move the inverse-video image; then hit the ENTER key), the program will ask you the problem name with up to six characters. Type "SAMPLE" and hit the ENTER key; then go to the next step. If you don't enter a problem name but only hit the ENTER key, the program will return to the function menu.

Step 4.   The general question about your LP model and some entry hints are shown on the screen. Now the cursor is on the first question. (Use the BACKSPACE key when you want to move the cursor back to the position if you have an error and reenter the correct data.)

4.1.   Your LP model is to maximize the objective function. Therefore, enter "1" and hit the ENTER key for the first question. The cursor will move down to the next question.

4.2.   Enter "4" and hit the ENTER key for the next question because your problem has four variables.

4.3.   Enter "3" and hit the ENTER key for the next question because your problem has three constraints.

4.4.   The default variable names are X1 to Xn. You will use "A" to "D" as the variable names, so enter "N." The program will automatically go to step 4.5.

4.5.   The message "Press the SPACE BAR to continue if your entries are correct." is shown at the bottom of the screen. If your entries are correct, press the SPACE BAR to go to the next entry form (step 5). Otherwise, hitting any key will move the cursor to the last question, and then the BACKSPACE key will move the cursor back to another question. Figure 3.5 shows these entries.

CHAPTER 3

```
Please observe the following conventions when entering a problem:
    (1) 100, 100.0, +100, +100.0, 1E2, and 1.0E+2 are the same.
    (2) -123, -1.23E2, and -1.23E+2 are the same.
    (3) >=, >, =>, and ≥ are the same; <=, <, =<, and ≤ are the same.
    (4) After you enter your data, press the ENTER key.
    (5) On the same screen page, you may correct errors by pressing
        the BACKSPACE key to move the cursor to the correct position.
    (6) When you are satisfied with the data on a page, press the SPACE BAR.
    (7) When entering the problem, press the Esc key to go to a previous
        page; press the / key to go to the next page.

Do you want to maximize (1) or minimize (2) criterion? (Enter 1 or 2)  <1 >

How many variables are there in your problem? (Enter number ≤ 40 )     <4 >

How many constraints are there in your problem? (Enter number ≤ 40 )   <3 >

Do you want to use the default variable names (X1,X2,...,Xn) (Y/N)?    <n >
```

FIGURE 3.5. Data entry for SAMPLE.

Step 5. <u>Enter the variable names</u>: Type each variable name up to four characters. If the variable name is less than four characters, you have to hit the ENTER key to move the cursor to the next entry field. If you don't enter any character for a variable name and only press the ENTER key, the program will automatically assign "Xn" as the variable name. Also, you can use the BACKSPACE key to move the cursor back to the position you want to change. After you finish entering variable names and make sure they are all right, press the SPACE BAR to go to the next step for model entry (step 6). Figure 3.6 shows these entries.

```
        Enter the variable names using at most 4 characters
    (To use default names, i.e., X1,X2,...,Xn, press the ENTER key)
       1 : <A   >    2 : <B   >    3 : <C   >    4 : <D   >
```

FIGURE 3.6. Variable names for SAMPLE.

Step 6. <u>Enter the LP model</u>: Now you have the LP model with blank coefficients on the screen. For every coefficient, you can enter up to eight digits. If you enter less than eight digits, press the ENTER key to move to the next coefficient. The directions of the constraints are defaulted by "≤" when the objective function is to maximize the criterion, and by "≥" for minimization. You can change them by typing ">", "> =", "<", "< =", or "=" when the cursor is on the fields of direction or by hitting the ENTER key to keep the default directions. Similarly, hitting the BACKSPACE key will move the cursor back to a previous entry field. Also, by pressing the "Esc" key the program will return to a previous page, and the "/" key will advance the program to the next page if the model has multiple pages. Note that you have to enter a large number by scientific format, such as "1.008e+8" for 100800000. Press the SPACE BAR when you finish entering the model and then hit any key to return to the function menu. Figure 3.7 shows these entries.

A Tutorial Guide to QSB

```
                   Enter the Coefficients of the LP Model      Page  1
   Max   4_____A    6_____B    3_____C    1_____D
   Subject to
   ( 1) 1.5_____A    2_____B    4_____C    3_____D    ≤ 550_____
   ( 2) 4_____A    1_____B    2_____C    1_____D    ≤ 700_____
   ( 3) 2_____A    3_____B    1_____C    2_____D    ≤ 300_____
```

FIGURE 3.7. Model entry of SAMPLE.

Step 7. Now the problem is in QSB. You can choose several options from the function menu at this time. If you want to display and/or print the problem, choose option 4 and then go to step 8. If you want to solve the problem, choose option 5 and go to step 9. To save the problem, choose option 6 and go to step 10. To modify the problem, select option 7 and go to step 11.

Step 8. <u>Display and/or print the input data</u>: As long as the problem is in the program, you can use this option to display or print it. This option will first ask whether you want to print the input data. If you do, hit the "Y" key; the input data will be displayed and printed at the same time. By hitting other keys, the input data will only be displayed. If the input data have multiple pages, hit the SPACE BAR to go to the next page.

Step 9. <u>Solve the problem</u>: You can solve the LP problem after you have entered or read it. The submenu to solve an LP problem is shown in Fig. 3.8. You may choose to display or not to display simplex tableaus. Suppose you choose option 4, which is to solve and display every tableau. The simplex tableaus will then be displayed sequentially on the screen as shown in Figs. 3.9 to 3.12. After displaying each tableau, you can hit the "G" key to skip the following tableaus or hit other keys to the next tableau. Note that tableau display is allowed only for small-scale problems. (Refer to Chapter 4 for more information.) After the problem has been solved, the program will automatically go to step 12 for displaying and/or printing the final solution.

```
                   Option Menu for Solving SAMPLE
      When solving the problem, you have the option to display steps of
   the simplex method.  This option is permissible only when your
   problem is small, that is, when N+N1+N2+N3*2 ≤ 9, where N is the
   number of variables, N1 is the number of '≤' constraints, N2 is the
   number of '='constraints, and N3 is the number of '≥'constraints;
   otherwise, only pivoting information will be displayed.

   Option
        1   ----   Solve and display the initial tableau
        2   ----   Solve and display the final tableau
        3   ----   Solve and display the initial and final tableaus
        4   ----   Solve and display every tableau
        5   ----   Solve without displaying any tableau
        6   ----   Return to the function menu
```

FIGURE 3.8. Solution menu for SAMPLE.

CHAPTER 3

Initial tableau

Basis	C(j)	A 4.000	B 6.000	C 3.000	D 1.000	S1 0	S2 0	S3 0	B(i)	B(i) A(i,j)
S1	0	1.500	2.000	4.000	3.000	1.000	0	0	550.0	0
S2	0	4.000	1.000	2.000	1.000	0	1.000	0	700.0	0
S3	0	2.000	3.000	1.000	2.000	0	0	1.000	300.0	0
C(j)-Z(j) * Big M		4.000 0	6.000 0	3.000 0	1.000 0	0 0	0 0	0 0	0 0	

FIGURE 3.9. Initial tableau for SAMPLE.

Iteration 1

Basis	C(j)	A 4.000	B 6.000	C 3.000	D 1.000	S1 0	S2 0	S3 0	B(i)	B(i) A(i,j)
S1	0	1.500	2.000	4.000	3.000	1.000	0	0	550.0	275.0
S2	0	4.000	1.000	2.000	1.000	0	1.000	0	700.0	700.0
S3	0	2.000	3.000	1.000	2.000	0	0	1.000	300.0	100.0
C(j)-Z(j) * Big M		4.000 0	6.000 0	3.000 0	1.000 0	0 0	0 0	0 0	0 0	

Current objective function value (Max.) = 0
< Highlighted variable is the entering or leaving variable >
Entering: B   Leaving: S3

FIGURE 3.10. First iteration for SAMPLE.

Iteration 2

Basis	C(j)	A 4.000	B 6.000	C 3.000	D 1.000	S1 0	S2 0	S3 0	B(i)	B(i) A(i,j)
S1	0	0.167	0	3.333	1.667	1.000	0	-.667	350.0	105.0
S2	0	3.333	0	1.667	0.333	0	1.000	-.333	600.0	360.0
B	6.000	0.667	1.000	0.333	0.667	0	0	0.333	100.0	300.0
C(j)-Z(j) * Big M		0 0	0 0	1.000 0	-3.00 0	0 0	0 0	-2.00 0	600.0 0	

Current objective function value (Max.) = 600
< Highlighted variable is the entering or leaving variable >
Entering: C   Leaving: S1

FIGURE 3.11. Second iteration for SAMPLE.

```
                 Final tableau (Total iteration=  2 )
       |        | A     | B     | C     | D     | S1    | S2    | S3    |       | B(i)
Basis  | C(j)   | 4.000 | 6.000 | 3.000 | 1.000 | 0     | 0     | 0     | B(i)  | A(i,j)
C      | 3.000  | 0.050 | 0     | 1.000 | 0.500 | 0.300 | 0     | -.200 | 105.0 | 0
S2     | 0      | 3.250 | 0     | 0     | -.500 | -.500 | 1.000 | 0     | 425.0 | 0
B      | 6.000  | 0.650 | 1.000 | 0     | 0.500 | -.100 | 0     | 0.400 | 65.00 | 0
C(j)-Z(j) |     | -.050 | 0     | 0     | -3.50 | -.300 | 0     | -1.80 | 705.0 |
 * Big M |      | 0     | 0     | 0     | 0     | 0     | 0     | 0     | 0     |

              (Max.) Optimal OBJ value =  705
```

FIGURE 3.12. Final tableau for SAMPLE.

Step 10. <u>Save the problem</u>: You may save the problem on any disk(ette) for later reference. Be sure the target disk(ette) is formatted. This option will ask you a file name to save your problem. If you just enter "A:", "B:", or "C:", the program will display the existing file names on the corresponding disk(ette) on A, B, or C drive. This will help you to check the existing file names. A file name with specified drive (A:, B:, or C:) will be saved on that specified disk(ette). The default drive is "A:". If you enter a file name that is already on the specified disk(ette), the program will ask if you want to replace it by the new data. Respond "Y" if you want to or press other keys if you don't want to.

Step 11. <u>Modify the problem</u>: If you find something wrong after you have entered the problem or want to change parameters of the problem, the LP program allows you to do many different modifications. The options to modify an LP model are shown in Fig. 3.13. For example, if you want to change an objective function coefficient, select option 1 from this submenu. The submenu also allows you to display and/or print the input data. After you finish all modifications, use option 8 from this submenu to go back to the function menu.

```
           Option Menu for Modifying SAMPLE
    Option
        1    ----   Modify the objective function coefficients
        2    ----   Modify one constraint
        3    ----   Add one constraint
        4    ----   Delete one constraint
        5    ----   Add one variable
        6    ----   Delete one variable
        7    ----   Display and/or print input data
        8    ----   Return to the function menu
```

FIGURE 3.13. Menu for modifying SAMPLE.

CHAPTER 3

Step 12. <u>Display and/or print the final solution</u>: After you have solved the problem, this function provides you with many options to display and/or print out the final solution. The options of this submenu are shown in Fig. 3.14. If you choose option 2, the summarized results and the sensitivity analysis for the objective function coefficients and the right-hand sides are as shown in Figs. 3.15 to 3.17.

```
Option Menu for Displaying and/or Printing the Final Solution to SAMPLE
        You have the following options available for displaying
     or printing the final solution.  If you want to print the
     solution, make sure that the printer is ready.

   Option
        1   ----  Display the final solution only
        2   ----  Display the solution and sensitivity analysis
        3   ----  Display/print the solution
        4   ----  Display/print the solution and sensitivity analysis
        5   ----  Return to the function menu
```

FIGURE 3.14. Menu for displaying final solution.

```
                 Summarized Results for SAMPLE      Page : 1
   Variables  |          | Opportunity | Variables |          | Opportunity
   No. Names  | Solution |    Cost     | No. Names | Solution |    Cost
   1    A         0.0000      0.0500     5    S1       0.0000      0.3000
   2    B        65.0000      0.0000     6    S2     425.0000      0.0000
   3    C       105.0000      0.0000     7    S3       0.0000      1.8000
   4    D         0.0000      3.5000
          Maximum value of the OBJ =   705    Iters.= 2
```

FIGURE 3.15. Summarized results for SAMPLE.

```
                 Sensitivity Analysis for OBJ Coefficients    Page : 1
   C(j) | Min. C(j) | Original | Max. C(j) | C(j) | Min. C(j) | Original | Max. C(j)
   C(1)   - Infinity   4.0000     4.0500    C(3)    2.0000     3.0000     12.0000
   C(2)     5.9231     6.0000     9.0000    C(4)  - Infinity   1.0000      4.5000
```

FIGURE 3.16. Sensitivity analysis for objective function coefficient.

```
                  Sensitivity Analysis for RHS          Page : 1
   B(i) | Min. B(i) | Original  | Max. B(i)  | B(i) | Min. B(i) | Original | Max. B(i)
   B(1)   200.0000    550.0000    1200.0000   B(3)   137.5000    300.0000    825.0000
   B(2)   275.0000    700.0000    + Infinity
```

FIGURE 3.17. Sensitivity analysis for right-hand sides of constraints.

Step 13. Read a problem: This is the function to read a previously saved problem. The question asks you to enter a file name for reading. If you forget the file name, you can only enter "A:", "B:", or "C:" to list all the files on the corresponding disk(ette). If you select a file name and enter it, but it is not on the specified disk(ette), the program will tell you it is not on that disk(ette). If the file is on the disk(ette), but the problem is not an LP problem, the program will tell you it is not an LP problem. You may reenter another name or return to the function menu.

Chapter 4
LINEAR PROGRAMMING (LP)

Overview of the LP Decision Support System

This program solves linear programming problems with up to 40 variables (not including slack/artificial variables) and 40 constraints. You should prepare the problem using the following format for data entry:

Maximize	3.2 GID1 + 4.0 GID2 − 5 GID3
Subject to:	4 GID1 + 2.5 GID2 + 3 GID3 ≤ 50
	3.6 GID1 + 7 GID2 − 2.5 GID3 ≤ 86.9
	15.7 GID1 + 9 GID3 = 20
	(variables are assumed to be nonnegative)

In this program, you can define variable names with up to four characters. Default variable names are X1, X2, ..., Xn. Problem entry is similar to your formulation. Any time you want a copy of the screen output, press the F8 key. You also have the option to print out the final solution and the sensitivity analysis. You can also display your problem and modify it if necessary. With LP, a problem can be saved on or read from a disk(ette). Furthermore, you can choose to display the detailed steps of the simplex method as the problem is solved.

Special Notes on the LP Program

1. When entering a problem, use the BACKSPACE key to move the cursor to the position where you want to make corrections.

2. The LP program uses the general simplex method to solve problems. In order to solve a problem with display of the entire tableau, You must have (N + N1 + N2 + 2 * N3) < 10, where N is the number of variables, N1 is the number of "less than or equal to" constraints, N2 is the number of "equality" constraints, and N3 is the number of "greater than or equal to" constraints. Otherwise, QSB will only display pivoting information.

3. "Big M" will be used when you have "equality" or "greater than or equal to" constraints in your problem. LP does not give M a specific value but treats it as a false number and keeps updating the coefficients of M in the objective function.

4. If the data in your problem have very different scales (e.g., 0.0001 and 10000), you should normalize some of the data. Otherwise, round-off errors may occur.

5. You may read an ILP file previously saved in the ILP program and solve it with the LP program. In this case, the bounds will be ignored.

6. All variables are assumed to be nonnegative. If you have some variables with negative values in your problem, you should transform them to nonnegative variables. Bounds are entered as normal constraints.

7. The slack and artificial variables are Sn and An, respectively, where n corresponds to the number of constraints.

8. Notation:

A(i,j):	Coefficient of constraint
B(i):	Right-hand side (RHS)
C(j):	Objective function coefficient
M:	Non-Archimedean large number
C(j)-Z(j):	Reduced cost (opportunity cost)

Solving Problems with LP

When you first select LP, the function menu, shown in Fig. 4.1, will appear. You can now select the appropriate option. The steps for using LP to solve a linear programming problem are listed below:

```
Welcome to your Linear Programming (LP) Decision Support System!
         The options available for LP are as follows.
  If you are a first-time user, you might benefit from option 1.

     Option                    Function

        1        ----    Overview of LP Decision Support System
        2        ----    Enter new problem
        3        ----    Read existing problem from disk(ette)
        4        ----    Display and/or print input data
        5        ----    Solve problem
        6        ----    Save problem on disk(ette)
        7        ----    Modify problem
        8        ----    Display and/or print final solution
        9        ----    Return to the program menu
        0        ----    Exit from QSB
```

FIGURE 4.1. Function menu of the LP program.

CHAPTER 4

1. Analyze the problem: define the decision variables.

2. Formulate an LP problem.

3. Enter the problem into QSB (use option 2) or read the existing problem from a data disk(ette) (use option 3).

4. Display or print the problem if you want to check and verify data (use option 4).

5. Modify the problem as necessary (use option 7).

6. Solve the problem by displaying or without displaying intermediate steps (use option 5).

7. Display and print the final solution (use option 8).

8. Save the problem on a data disk(ette) if you may need it again (use option 6).

9. If you want to solve other problems, go to step 3. Otherwise, return to the program menu (use option 9) to select another program or exit from QSB (use option zero).

Example

To demonstrate the use of LP, consider the following example problem. Austin Manufacturing Company (AMC) has two machines to make products A and B. Each product requires operation times on each machine. Table 4.1 shows these operation requirements and the total available times on both machines in one month. Considering the current market, AMC can sell as much as it can produce of products A and B. The market prices for each product are $50 and $60, respectively. Management would like to determine the best production plan for AMC so as to maximize total revenues for the coming month.

Table 4.1. Unit operation requirements and machine capacities (in hours)

Machine	Product A	Product B	Total capacity for one month
1	2	3	180
2	3	2	150

Step 1. Define decision variables:

Let A = number of product A produced in one month
    B = number of product B produced in one month

Linear Programming

Step 2. Formulate the LP problem as follows:

Maximize   50 A + 60 B

Subject to: 2 A + 3 B ≤ 180
3 A + 2 B ≤ 150
A, B ≥ 0

Step 3. Enter the problem (the data underlined in the following figures will be entered into LP):

3.1. Enter problem name AMC.

3.2. Enter the information shown in Fig. 4.2 to define the problem. Note the conventions that appear on the screen when you enter data.

```
Please observe the following conventions when entering a problem:
  (1) 100, 100.0, +100, +100.0, 1E2, and 1.0E+2 are the same.
  (2) -123, -1.23E2, and -1.23E+2 are the same.
  (3) >=, >, =>, and ≥ are the same; <=, <, =<, and ≤ are the same.
  (4) After you enter your data, press the ENTER key.
  (5) On the same screen page, you may correct errors by pressing
      the BACKSPACE key to move the cursor to the correct position.
  (6) When you are satisfied with the data on a page, press the SPACE BAR.
  (7) When entering the problem, press the Esc key to go to a previous
      page; press the / key to go to the next page.

Do you want to maximize (1) or minimize (2) criterion? (Enter 1 or 2)  <1 >

How many variables are there in your problem? (Enter number ≤ 40 )   <2 >

How many constraints are there in your problem? (Enter number ≤ 40 )  <2 >

Do you want to use the default variable names (X1,X2,...,Xn) (Y/N)?  <n >
```

FIGURE 4.2. Screen display of LP for defining a problem.

3.3. Figure 4.3 displays the screen for defining the names of variables. Note that we could use default names (X1 and X2). After entering the names, press the SPACE BAR.

```
        Enter the variable names using at most 4 characters
    (To use default names, i.e., X1,X2,...,Xn, press the ENTER key)

     1 : <A   >    2 : <B   >
```

FIGURE 4.3. Screen display for defining variable names.

3.4. Figure 4.4 displays the screen for entering the coefficients of the objective function and constraints. After entering each coefficient, press the ENTER key.

CHAPTER 4

```
                 Enter the Coefficients of the LP Model      Page   1

Max    50_____A     60_____B
Subject to
( 1)    2_____A      3_____B    ≤  180_____
( 2)    3_____A      2_____B    ≤  150_____
```

FIGURE 4.4. Screen display for entering an LP problem.

Step 4. You may display or print the problem, as shown in Fig. 4.5.

```
Max    +50.0000A    +60.0000B
Subject to
( 1)   +2.00000A    +3.00000B    ≤  +180.000
( 2)   +3.00000A    +2.00000B    ≤  +150.000
```

FIGURE 4.5. Screen display of the problem for AMC.

Step 5. You have the option of modifying the problem as needed. This gives the menu displayed in Fig. 4.6.

```
                       Option Menu for Modifying AMC

        Option

             1   ----   Modify the objective function coefficients
             2   ----   Modify one constraint
             3   ----   Add one constraint
             4   ----   Delete one constraint
             5   ----   Add one variable
             6   ----   Delete one variable
             7   ----   Display and/or print input data
             8   ----   Return to the function menu
```

FIGURE 4.6. Option menu for modifying an LP problem.

Step 6. You are now ready to solve the problem. Select option 5 from the function menu to call up the solution menu displayed in Fig. 4.7. Note that if you select option 5 from the solution menu, you will see every iteration on the screen. These iterations are shown in Figs. 4.8 to 4.11.

```
                    Option Menu for Solving AMC
   When solving the problem, you have the option to display steps of
the simplex method.  This option is permissible only when your
problem is small, that is, when N+N1+N2+N3*2 ≤ 9, where N is the
number of variables, N1 is the number of '≤' constraints, N2 is the
number of '=' constraints, and N3 is the number of '≥' constraints;
otherwise, only pivoting information will be displayed.

 Option

   1    ----    Solve and display the initial tableau
   2    ----    Solve and display the final tableau
   3    ----    Solve and display the initial and final tableaus
   4    ----    Solve and display every tableau
   5    ----    Solve without displaying any tableau
   6    ----    Return to the function menu
```

FIGURE 4.7. Option menu for solving an LP problem.

Initial tableau

		A	B	S1	S2		B(i)
Basis	C(j)	50.00	60.00	0	0	B(i)	A(i,j)
S1	0	2.000	3.000	1.000	0	180.0	0
S2	0	3.000	2.000	0	1.000	150.0	0
C(j)-Z(j)		50.00	60.00	0	0	0	
* Big M		0	0	0	0	0	

FIGURE 4.8. The initial simplex tableau for the AMC problem.

Iteration 1

		A	B	S1	S2		B(i)
Basis	C(j)	50.00	60.00	0	0	B(i)	A(i,j)
S1	0	2.000	3.000	1.000	0	180.0	60.00
S2	0	3.000	2.000	0	1.000	150.0	75.00
C(j)-Z(j)		50.00	60.00	0	0	0	
* Big M		0	0	0	0	0	

```
         Current objective function value (Max.) =  0
   < Highlighted variable is the entering or leaving variable >
              Entering: B    Leaving: S1
```

FIGURE 4.9. The simplex tableau of the first iteration for the AMC problem.

CHAPTER 4

```
            Iteration  2
```

		A	B	S1	S2		B(i)
Basis	C(j)	50.00	60.00	0	0	B(i)	A(i,j)
B	60.00	0.667	1.000	0.333	0	60.00	90.00
S2	0	1.667	0	-.667	1.000	30.00	18.00
C(j)-Z(j)		10.00	0	-20.0	0	3600	
* Big M		0	0	0	0	0	

```
       Current objective function value (Max.) =  3600
    < Highlighted variable is the entering or leaving variable >
                   Entering: A    Leaving: S2
```

FIGURE 4.10. The simplex tableau of the second iteration for the AMC problem.

```
         Final tableau (Total iteration=  2 )
```

		A	B	S1	S2		B(i)
Basis	C(j)	50.00	60.00	0	0	B(i)	A(i,j)
B	60.00	0	1.000	0.600	-.400	48.00	0
A	50.00	1.000	0	-.400	0.600	18.00	0
C(j)-Z(j)		0	0	-16.0	-6.00	3780	
* Big M		0	0	0	0	0	

```
         (Max.) Optimal OBJ value =  3780
```

FIGURE 4.11. The simplex tableau of the final iteration for the AMC problem.

Step 7. After the problem has been solved, you may use option 8 in the function menu to display or print the final solution. The menu of options available for displaying or printing is shown in Fig. 4.12. If option 4 is chosen from this menu, the final solution and sensitivity analyses are displayed and automatically printed, as shown in Figs. 4.13 to 4.15.

```
Option Menu for Displaying and/or Printing the Final Solution to AMC
      You have the following options available for displaying
      or printing the final solution.  If you want to print the
      solution, make sure that the printer is ready.

 Option

     1   ----   Display the final solution only
     2   ----   Display the solution and sensitivity analysis
     3   ----   Display/print the solution
     4   ----   Display/print the solution and sensitivity analysis
     5   ----   Return to the function menu
```

FIGURE 4.12. Option menu for displaying and printing LP solution.

Linear Programming

	Summarized Results for AMC		Page : 1			
Variables No. Names	Solution	Opportunity Cost	Variables No. Names	Solution	Opportunity Cost
1 A	18.0000	0.0000	3 S1	0.0000	16.0000
2 B	48.0000	0.0000	4 S2	0.0000	6.0000
Maximum value of the OBJ = 3780   Iters.= 2

FIGURE 4.13. Final solution for the AMC problem.

Sensitivity Analysis for OBJ Coefficients						Page : 1	
C(j)	Min. C(j)	Original	Max. C(j)	C(j)	Min. C(j)	Original	Max. C(j)
C(1)	40.0000	50.0000	90.0000	C(2)	33.3333	60.0000	75.0000

FIGURE 4.14. Sensitivity analysis of OBJ for the AMC problem.

Sensitivity Analysis for RHS						Page : 1	
B(i)	Min. B(i)	Original	Max. B(i)	B(i)	Min. B(i)	Original	Max. B(i)
B(1)	100.0000	180.0000	225.0000	B(2)	120.0000	150.0000	270.0000

FIGURE 4.15. Sensitivity analysis for RHS for the AMC problem.

Step 8. By choosing option 6 from the function menu, you can save the problem on a data disk(ette). Make sure that your data disk(ette) is formatted and inserted in the disk(ette) drive. Figure 4.16 gives the screen display for saving your problem.

```
                Save Problem on Disk(ette)
        Decide on a file name for saving your problem.
         The file name may be the same as the problem name.
        Type x:xxxxxxxx.xxx for your file name ( e.g., A:XYZ.DAT ).
What is your file name (Type A:, B:, or C: to see all the files) ? a:AMCFILE.dat
```

FIGURE 4.16. Screen display for saving a problem.

The Big M Method—An Example

If the problem contains "equality" (=) or "greater than or equal to" ($\geq$) constraints, the LP program uses the Big M method to solve the problem. (An artificial variable is generated for each" = " or "$\geq$" constraint and a corresponding M coefficient is added

29

CHAPTER 4

to the objective function.) The following example (named BIGMEX) contains two "⩾" constraints, and Fig. 4.17 shows the simplex tableau of the first iteration for this problem. The artificial variables and the coefficients of M are pointed out in the figure. Also, Figs. 4.18 to 4.20 show the final solution and sensitivity analyses for this example problem.

Minimize $2.5\ X1 + 2\ X2$

Subject to: $6\ X1 + 3\ X2 \geqslant 100$
$3\ X1 + 5\ X2 \geqslant 120$
$X1, X2 \geqslant 0$

Iteration 1

Basis	C(j)	X1	X2	S1	A1 *	S2	A2 *	B(i)	B(i)/A(i,j)
		2.500	2.000	0	M	0	M		
A1	M	6.000	3.000	-1.00	1.000	0	0	100.0	16.67
A2	M	3.000	5.000	0	0	-1.00	1.000	120.0	40.00
C(j)-Z(j)		2.500	2.000	0	0	0	0	0	
* Big M		†-9.00	†-8.00	1.000	0	†1.000	0	220.0	

Current objective function value (Min.) = 0 + (220 Big M)
< Highlighted variable is the entering or leaving variable >
Entering: X1   Leaving: A1
*Artificial variables   †Coefficient of M

FIGURE 4.17. The first iteration of example with Big M method.

Summarized Results for BIGMEX   Page : 1

Variables No. Names	Solution	Opportunity Cost	Variables No. Names	Solution	Opportunity Cost
1 X1	6.6667	0.0000	4 A1	0.0000	-0.3095
2 X2	20.0000	0.0000	5 S2	0.0000	0.2143
3 S1	0.0000	0.3095	6 A2	0.0000	-0.2143

Minimum value of the OBJ = 56.66666   Iters.= 2

FIGURE 4.18. The final solution of example with Big M method.

Sensitivity Analysis for OBJ Coefficients   Page : 1

C(j)	Min. C(j)	Original	Max. C(j)	C(j)	Min. C(j)	Original	Max. C(j)
C(1)	1.2000	2.5000	4.0000	C(2)	1.2500	2.0000	4.1667

FIGURE 4.19. Sensitivity analysis of OBJ of example with Big M method.

		Sensitivity Analysis for RHS			Page : 1		
B(i)	Min. B(i)	Original	Max. B(i)	B(i)	Min. B(i)	Original	Max. B(i)
B(1)	72.0000	100.0000	240.0000	B(2)	50.0000	120.0000	166.6667

FIGURE 4.20. Sensitivity analysis of RHS example with Big M method.

Exercises

1. Consider the following LP problem:

   Maximize $8 X_1 + 12 X_2$

   Subject to: $2 X_1 + 5 X_2 \leq 250$
   $11 X_1 + 9 X_2 \leq 710$
   for $X_1, X_2 \geq 0$

   a. Find the optimal solution.
   b. What are the ranges of optimality for the coefficients of the objective function and the right-hand sides?

2. Consider the following LP model:

   Minimize $A + 3 B - 4 C$

   Subject to: $A + B \leq 150$
   $3 A + 2 B - C \geq 210$
   $5 A - 2 B + 4 C \geq 315$
   for A, B, and $C \geq 0$

   a. Find the optimal solution.
   b. What is the opportunity cost for each constraint?

3. Find the optimal solution for the following LP problem:

   Maximize $7 X_1 + 9 X_2 - 3 X_3 + 11 X_4 - X_5 + 2 X_6$

   Subject to: $X_1 + X_2 + X_3 + X_4 + X_5 + X_6 \leq 200$
   $2 X_1 + 2 X_2 + 6 X_3 - X_4 + 2 X_5 + 7 X_6 \geq 271$
   $4 X_1 + 2 X_3 + 3 X_5 - X_6 \leq 350$
   $7 X_2 + 11 X_3 - 4 X_4 + 6 X_5 \leq 429$
   $X_1 + 4 X_3 + 7 X_5 \leq 310$
   for $X_1, X_2, X_3, X_4, X_5,$ and $X_6 \geq 0$

4. Full Speed, Inc., produces three industrial parts from raw materials A and B. One unit of part X requires four units of A and three units of B; one unit of part Y

CHAPTER 4

requires seven units of A and two units of B; and one unit of Z requires three units of A and eight units of B. Transportation problems have restricted the company to get, at most, 1700 units of material A and 1500 units of material B each month. The company has contracts on hand to supply at least 50 units of part X, 50 units of part Y, and 70 units of part Z. Industries can consume as much as the company produces. If the unit profits for parts X, Y, and Z are $15, $20, and $21, respectively, what is the best production plan for Full Speed to obtain maximum profit?

5. Midwestern Airline has its headquarters in a northwestern city. During the summer, the company business increases substantially because of vacation travelers. Currently, Midwestern has an online reservation system. The following table lists the reservation clerk requirements by two-hour periods during the day.

Period	Time		Clerks required
1	6 A.M. to	8 A.M.	3
2	8 A.M. to	10 A.M.	12
3	10 A.M. to	12 A.M.	13
4	12 A.M. to	2 P.M.	10
5	2 P.M. to	4 P.M.	12
6	4 P.M. to	6 P.M.	10
7	6 P.M. to	8 P.M.	6
8	8 P.M. to	10 P.M.	5
9	10 P.M. to	midnight	4
10	midnight to	2 A.M.	3

The company plans to use six work shifts, as shown below, including two split shifts.

Shift	Times
1	6 A.M. to 2 P.M.
2	8 A.M. to 4 P.M.
3	10 A.M. to 6 P.M.
4	6 P.M. to 2 A.M.
5	10 A.M. to 1 P.M. and 4 P.M. to 8 P.M.
6	8 A.M. to 11 A.M. and 5 P.M. to 9 P.M.

Formulate an LP problem to determine the minimal number of reservation clerks required. Use QSB to solve it.

6. Sesame Oil Company produces three grades of motor oil: regular, high power, and super power. They are blended from three types of crude oil. Each type of crude oil contains three important ingredients. The percentages of ingredients in each type of crude oil are shown below:

Crude oil/ingredient	I	II	III
A	80%	10%	5%
B	45%	30%	20%
C	30%	40%	25%

The specifications of the three types of motor oil are as follows:

Motor oil/ingredient	I	II	III
Super power	$\geqslant 60\%$	$\leqslant 25\%$	$\leqslant 10\%$
High power	$\geqslant 50\%$	$\leqslant 30\%$	$\leqslant 15\%$
Regular	$\leqslant 40\%$	$\geqslant 35\%$	$\geqslant 20\%$

The costs per gallon for crude oil A, B, and C are $0.65, $0.5, and $0.45, respectively. Daily demands for super power, high power, and regular are at least 50,000 gallons, 70,000 gallons, and 40,000 gallons. Establish a good blending plan for Sesame Oil. In other words, determine how many gallons of each type of crude oil should be used in each type of motor oil.

Chapter 5
INTEGER LINEAR PROGRAMMING (ILP)

Overview of the ILP Decision Support System

This program solves mixed integer linear programming problems with up to 20 variables (not including slack/artificial variables) and 20 constraints (not including bounds) by using the branch-and-bound method. Prepare your problems by using the following format for data entry:

Maximize $3.2\ GID1 + 4.0\ GID2 - 5\ GID3$

Subject to: $4\ GID1 + 2.5\ GID2 + 3\ GID3 \leq 50$
$3.6\ GID1 + 7\ GID2 - 2.5\ GID3 \leq 86.9$

Bounds: $GID1 \leq 2$, and is integral.
(variables are assumed to be nonnegative)

In this program, you can define variable names with up to four characters. Default variable names are X1, X2, ..., Xn. The entry of the model follows your formulation. Any time you want a copy of the screen output, press the F8 key. You also have the option of printing the final solution. The program allows you to display your problem and to modify it as necessary. With ILP, the problem can be saved on and read from any disk(ette). Furthermore, you can also choose to display the detailed steps of the branch-and-bound method as the problem is being solved.

Special Notes on the ILP Program

1. When entering a problem, use the BACKSPACE key to move the cursor to the position where you want to make corrections.

2. The ILP program uses the branch-and-bound method to solve mixed integer linear programming problems. The ILP can solve problems with up to 20 variables (not including slack or artificial variables) and 20 constraints(not including bounds). Bounds of variables are defined separately. When entering data, you need to enter constraints and bounds separately. The variables may be integral, zero-one value, or real.

3. When solving a problem, you can display each branch-and-bound iteration.

4. If the data in your problem have very different scales (e.g., 0.0001 and 10000), you should normalize some of the data. Otherwise, round-off errors may occur.

Integer Linear Programming

5. You may read an LP file previously saved in the LP program and solve it by the ILP program. In this case, you may define bounds and integrality after the problem has been read.

6. All variables are assumed to be nonnegative. If variables with negative values are in your problem, you should transform them to nonnegative variables.

Solving Problems with ILP

When you first select ILP, the function menu, shown in Fig. 5.1, will appear. You can now select the appropriate option. The steps for using ILP to solve mixed integer linear programming problems are listed below:

```
Welcome to your Integer Linear Programming (ILP) Decision Support System!
            The options available for ILP are as follows.
   If you are a first-time user, you might benefit from option 1.

     Option                      Function

        1          ----    Overview of ILP Decision Support System
        2          ----    Enter new problem
        3          ----    Read existing problem from disk(ette)
        4          ----    Display and/or print input data
        5          ----    Solve problem
        6          ----    Save problem on disk(ette)
        7          ----    Modify problem
        8          ----    Display and/or print final solution
        9          ----    Return to the program menu
        0          ----    Exit from QSB
```

FIGURE 5.1. Function menu of the ILP program.

1. Analyze the problem: define decision variables.

2. Formulate an LP problem and specify integrality and bounds of variables.

3. Enter the problem into QSB (use option 2) or read the existing problem from a data disk(ette) (use option 3).

4. Display or print the problem if you want to check and verify data (use option 4).

5. Modify the problem as necessary (use option 7).

6. Solve the problem by displaying or without displaying intermediate steps (use option 5).

7. Display and print the final solution (use option 8).

CHAPTER 5

8. Save the problem on a data disk(ette) if you may need it again (use option 6).

9. If you want to solve other problems, go to step 3. Otherwise return to the program menu (use option 9) to select another program or exit from QSB (use option 0).

Example

To demonstrate the use of ILP, consider the following example problem. A nutrition plan requires at least 200 units of protein and 180 units of fat. Chemical analyses have shown that 1 unit of food A contains 6 units of protein and 3 units of fat, and 1 unit of food B contains 3 units of protein and 5 units of fat. The sales of these two types of food are in whole units with unit prices of $2.50 for A and $2 for B. What is the combination that will satisfy the required nutrition levels and at the same time minimize total cost?

Step 1. Define decision variables:

Let X_a = number of units of food A used.
    X_b = number of units of food B used.

Step 2. Formulate an LP problem and specify bounds and integrality:

$$\text{Minimize } 2.5 X_a + 2 X_b$$
$$\text{Subject to: } 6 X_a + 3 X_b \geq 200$$
$$3 X_a + 5 X_b \geq 180$$
$$X_a, X_b \geq 0 \text{ and are integers}$$

```
Please observe the following conventions when entering a problem:

(1) 100, 100.0, +100, +100.0, 1E2, and 1.0E+2 are the same.
(2) -123, -1.23E2, and -1.23E+2 are the same.
(3) >=, >, =>, and ≥ are the same; <=, <, =<, and ≤ are the same.
(4) After you enter your data, press the ENTER key.
(5) On the same screen page, you may correct errors by pressing
    the BACKSPACE key to move the cursor to the correct position.
(6) When you are satisfied with the data on a page, press the SPACE BAR.
(7) When entering the problem, press the Esc key to go to a previous
    page; press the / key to go to the next page.

Do you want to maximize (1) or minimize (2) criterion? (Enter 1 or 2)   <2 >

How many variables are there in your problem? (Enter number ≤ 20 )      <2 >

How many constraints are there in your problem? (Enter number ≤ 20 )    <2 >

Do you want to use the default variable names (X1,X2,...,Xn) (Y/N)?     <n >
```

FIGURE 5.2. Screen display of ILP for defining a problem.

Integer Linear Programming

Step 3. Enter the problem (the data underlined in the following figures will be entered into ILP):

3.1. Enter problem name NUTRI.

3.2. Enter the information shown in Fig. 5.2 to define the problem. Note the conventions that appear on the screen when you enter data.

3.3. Figure 5.3 displays the screen for defining the names of variables. Note that we could use default names (X1 and X2). After entering the names, press the SPACE BAR.

```
            Enter variable names using at most 4 characters
      (To use default names, i.e., X1,X2,...,Xn, press the ENTER key)
         1 : <Xa  >     2 : <Xb  >
```
FIGURE 5.3. Screen display for defining variable names.

3.4. Figures 5.4 and 5.5 display the screens for defining the integrality and bounds of variables. Note that the upper bound of an integral variable is 32000.

```
                Enter Integrality and Bounds for Variables

Are all variables integer (Y/N)?y

Are all variables with 0-1 values (Y/N)?n

Are you going to define bounds for variables (Y/N)?
```
FIGURE 5.4. Screen display for specifying integrality.

```
                 Enter Integrality and Bounds for Variables
       (Default values are continuous with lower bound 0 and upper bound 32000)
            Var.\no.   Var.   Integrality (I/C)   Lower bound      Upper bound
               1        Xa         <I>               <0     >       <1000   >
               2        Xb         <I>               <0     >       <1000   >
```
FIGURE 5.5. Screen display for defining integrality and bounds.

3.5. Figure 5.6 displays the screen for entering the coefficients of the objective function and constraints. Note that you may change the default directions of constraints. After entering each coefficient, press the ENTER key.

CHAPTER 5

```
                    Entering the Coefficients of ILP Model
Min  2.5_____Xa  2_____Xb
Subject to
( 1)  6_____Xa  3_____Xb  ≥  200_____
( 2)  3_____Xa  5_____Xb  ≥  180_____
```

FIGURE 5.6. Screen display for entering an ILP model.

Step 4. You may display or print the problem, as shown in Fig. 5.7.

```
                    Input Data Describing Your Problem NUTRI
Min  +2.50000Xa  +2.00000Xb
Subject to
( 1) +6.00000Xa  +3.00000Xb  ≥  +200.000
( 2) +3.00000Xa  +5.00000Xb  ≥  +180.000
                    Integrality and Bounds for Variables
(Default values are continuous with lower bound 0 and upper bound 32000)

    Var. no.   Var.   Integrality (I/C)   Lower bound      Upper bound
       1        Xa         <I>              <0      >        <1000    >
       2        Xb         <I>              <0      >        <1000    >
```

FIGURE 5.7. Screen display of the problem for Nutri.

Step 5. You have the option of modifying the problem as needed. This gives the menu displayed in Fig. 5.8.

```
┌──────────────────────────────────────────────────────────────────┐
│                    Option Menu for Modifying NUTRI               │
├──────────────────────────────────────────────────────────────────┤
│      Option                                                      │
│                                                                  │
│         1    ----   Modify the objective function coefficients   │
│         2    ----   Modify constraint                            │
│         3    ----   Add one constraint                           │
│         4    ----   Delete one constraint                        │
│         5    ----   Add one variable                             │
│         6    ----   Delete one variable                          │
│         7    ----   Modify integrality and bounds                │
│         8    ----   Display and/or print input data              │
│         9    ----   Return to the function menu                  │
│                                                                  │
└──────────────────────────────────────────────────────────────────┘
```

FIGURE 5.8. Option menu for modifying an ILP problem.

Step 6. You are now ready to solve the problem. Select option 5 from the function menu. This will call up the solution menu displayed in Fig. 5.9. Note that if you se-

Integer Linear Programming

lect option 2 from the solution menu, you will see every iteration on the screen. These iterations are shown in Figs. 5.10 to 5.14.

```
                    Option Menu for Solving NUTRI
           When solving a problem, you have the option of displaying
           every iteration of the branch-and-bound solution.
 Option
     1    ----   Solve and display the first iteration
     2    ----   Solve and display each iteration
     3    ----   Solve without displaying any iteration
     4    ----   Change integer tolerance (default tolerance is .001)
     5    ----   Return to the function menu
```

FIGURE 5.9. Option menu for solving an ILP problem.

```
 Current Branch-and-Bound Solution--Iteration: 1   Page: 1
 Lw. bound | Variable | Up. bound | Variable | Solution | Obj. Fnctn.
     0   ≤     Xa      ≤  1000       Xa         21.905      2.500
     0   ≤     Xb      ≤  1000       Xb         22.857      2.000
 Noninteger solution with OBJ (Min.) = 100.4762   ZU = 1E+20
```

FIGURE 5.10. The first iteration for the Nutri problem.

```
 Current Branch-and-Bound Solution--Iteration: 2   Page: 1
 Lw. bound | Variable | Up. bound | Variable | Solution | Obj. Fnctn.
    22   ≤     Xa      ≤  1000       Xa         22.000      2.500
     0   ≤     Xb      ≤  1000       Xb         22.800      2.000
 Noninteger solution with OBJ (Min.) = 100.6   ZU = 1E+20
```

FIGURE 5.11. The second iteration for the Nutri problem.

```
 Current Branch-and-Bound Solution--Iteration: 3   Page: 1
 Lw. bound | Variable | Up. bound | Variable | Solution | Obj. Fnctn.
    22   ≤     Xa      ≤  1000       Xa         22.000      2.500
    23   ≤     Xb      ≤  1000       Xb         23.000      2.000
 Integer feasible solution with OBJ (Min.) = 101 ≤ ZU = 1E+20
```

FIGURE 5.12. The third iteration for the Nutri problem.

39

CHAPTER 5

```
Current Branch-and-Bound Solution--Iteration: 4   Page: 1
Lw. bound │ Variable │ Up. bound │ Variable │ Solution │ Obj. Fnctn.
    22    ≤    Xa    ≤  1000    │    Xa    │  23.333  │   2.500
     0    ≤    Xb    ≤    22    │    Xb    │  22.000  │   2.000
         Current OBJ (Min.) = 102.3333 ≥ ZU = 101
```

FIGURE 5.13. The fourth iteration for the Nutri problem.

```
Current Branch-and-Bound Solution--Iteration: 5   Page: 1
Lw. bound │ Variable │ Up. bound │ Variable │ Solution │ Obj. Fnctn.
     0    ≤    Xa    ≤    21    │    Xa    │  21.000  │   2.500
     0    ≤    Xb    ≤  1000    │    Xb    │  24.667  │   2.000
         Current OBJ (Min.) = 101.8333 ≥ ZU = 101
```

FIGURE 5.14. The fifth iteration for the Nutri problem.

Step 7. After the problem has been solved, we may use option 8 in the function menu to display or print the final solution. The menu of options available for displaying or printing is shown in Fig. 5.15. If we choose option 2 from this menu, the final solution is displayed and automatically printed, as shown in Fig. 5.16.

```
Option Menu for Displaying and/or Printing the Final Solution to NUTRI
        You have the following options available for displaying
     or printing the final solution. If you want to print the
     solution, make sure that the printer is ready.

         Option
           1   ----  Display the final solution only
           2   ----  Display and print the final solution
           3   ----  Return to the function menu
```

FIGURE 5.15. Option menu for displaying and printing final solution.

```
              Summary of Results for NUTRI    Page : 1
Variables │           │ Obj. Fnctn. │ Variables │          │ Obj. Fnctn.
No. Names │ Solution  │ Coefficient │ No. Names │ Solution │ Coefficient
   1  Xa  │  22.000   │    2.500    │   2  Xb   │  23.000  │    2.000
     Minimum value of the OBJ = 101   Total iterations = 5
```

FIGURE 5.16. The final solution for the Nutri problem.

Integer Linear Programming

Step 8. By choosing option 6 from the function menu, you can save the problem on a data disk(ette). Make sure that your data disk(ette) is formatted and inserted in the disk(ette) drive. Figure 5.17 gives the screen display for saving your problem.

```
                    Save Problem on Disk(ette)
           Decide on a file name for saving your problem.
           The file name may be the same as the problem name.
        Type x:xxxxxxxx.xxx for your file name ( e.g., A:XYZ.DAT ).
What is your file name (Type A:, B:, or C: to see all the files) ? a:NUTRI.dat
```

FIGURE 5.17. Screen display for saving the Nutri problem.

0-1 Integer Linear Programming Problem

The following example demonstrates a 0-1 integer linear programming problem.

    Maximize $10 X_1 + 20 X_2 + 15 X_3$

    Subject to: $X_1 + X_2 + X_3 \leq 2$
                      $2 X_1 + 6 X_2 + 4 X_3 \leq 9$
                      $X_1, X_2, X_3 = 0$, or 1

Data entry with ILP is shown in Figs. 5.18 to 5.20; the final solution is shown in Fig. 5.21.

```
                    ILP Model Entry for PURE01

Please observe the following conventions when entering a problem:
    (1) 100, 100.0, +100, +100.0, 1E2, and 1.0E+2 are the same.
    (2) -123, -1.23E2, and -1.23E+2 are the same.
    (3) >=, >, =>, and ≥ are the same; <=, <, =<, and ≤ are the same.
    (4) After you enter your data, press the ENTER key.
    (5) On the same screen page, you may correct errors by pressing
        the BACKSPACE key to move the cursor to the correct position.
    (6) When you are satisfied with the data on a page, press the SPACE BAR.
    (7) When entering the problem, press the Esc key to go to a previous
        page; press the / key to go to the next page.
Do you want to maximize (1) or minimize (2) criterion? (Enter 1 or 2)   <1 >
How many variables are there in your problem? (Enter number ≤ 20 )      <3 >
How many constraints are there in your problem? (Enter number ≤ 20 )    <2 >
Do you want to use the default variable names (X1,X2,...,Xn) (Y/N)?     <y >
```

FIGURE 5.18. Screen display for defining an ILP problem.

CHAPTER 5

```
              Enter Integrality and Bounds for Variables

 Are all variables integer (Y/N)?y

 Are all variables with 0-1 values (Y/N)?
```

FIGURE 5.19. Screen display for defining 0-1 variables.

```
              Entering the Coefficients of ILP Model
Max   10_____X1   20_____X2   15_____X3
Subject to
( 1)  1_____X1   1_____X2   1_____X3  ≤  2_____
( 2)  2_____X1   6_____X2   4_____X3  ≤  9_____
```

FIGURE 5.20. Screen display for entering an ILP problem.

```
                  Summary of Results for PURE01        Page : 1
 |Variables|          |Obj. Fnctn. |Variables|          |Obj. Fnctn.
 |No. Names| Solution |Coefficient |No. Names| Solution |Coefficient
 |1   X1   |  1.000   |  10.000    | 3   X3  |  0.000   |  15.000
 |2   X2   |  1.000   |  20.000    |
            Maximum value of the OBJ =  30   Total iterations = 7
```

FIGURE 5.21. The final solution for the 0-1 problem.

Exercises

1. Assume that X1 and X2 are integral with the upper bound 40 and lower bound 30 for problem 1 in Chapter 4. Solve the problem by the ILP program and observe each branch.

2. Assume that all variables for problem 3 in Chapter 4 are integral with no bounds. Solve the problem by the ILP program.

3. Solve the following problem by ILP. Observe each iteration and draw a branch-and-bound tree.

    Maximize   2 X1 + X2

    Subject to: 2 X1 + 2 X2 ≤ 8
                 4 X1 +   X2 ≤ 8
                 X1, X2 ⩾ 0 and integer

4. Consider a capital budgeting problem in which five possible projects are being considered for implementation over the next three years. The expected returns for each project, the annual expenditures, and budget (all in thousands of dollars)

are shown in the table. Assume that each approved project will continue over the entire three-year period.

Project	Year 1	Expenditures Year 2	Year 3	Expected return
1	5	1	8	22
2	4	7	10	40
3	3	9	2	25
4	7	4	1	16
5	8	6	10	28
Budget	22	25	30	

  a. Formulate a zero-one integer linear programming model to maximize the total expected returns. Assume that unused funds cannot be carried forward. Use the ILP program to find the best solution.
  b. When project 5 is selected, then either project 1 or project 2 may be selected, but not both. Add this constraint and resolve it.

5. Midwestern Public Utility must expand its electrical generation capacity by at least 1500 million kilowatts. It can do so in one or more of the following ways:
   a. A conventional coal-fire plant could be built but must be located adjacent to a railroad right-of-way to facilitate the delivery of coal. Because of the desirability of land near existing railroad tracks, a suitable plant site will cost $2 million. The cost of building a conventional plant (exclusive of site costs) is estimated to be $0.5 million per million kilowatts of generating capacity.
   b. A nuclear plant could be built but must be located in a remote area for safety. A suitable site for a nuclear plant can be obtained for $1 million. The cost of constructing the nuclear plant, exclusive of the site cost, is estimated to be $0.8 million per million kilowatts of generating capacity.
   c. Due to recently passed legislation, a dam on a nearby river could be built. The dam will cost $4 million, but an attendant hydroelectric plant can be built at a cost of $0.1 million per million kilowatts of generating capacity. Unfortunately, the maximum capacity for such a plant is only 400 million kilowatts; moreover, if a dam is built, Consolidated must also agree to build a nuclear power plant.

Formulate an integer linear programming model to decide the least expensive means to expand the generating capacity by at least 1500 million kilowatts. Use the ILP program to solve it. Do you find any unreasonable conditions from the solution?

6. The CMC Company is opening a major research center in Austin, and it must purchase 400 desks for its offices. Three vendors in the area sell large volumes of desks. Vendor I can supply any number of desks for $500 each, plus a fixed order cost of $100. Vendor II can supply up to 350 desks. The first 100 desks will cost $550 each, while any additional desks over 100 will cost $490 each. There is no

CHAPTER 5

fixed ordering cost. Vendor III has a minimum order quantity of 50 desks and a maximum order quantity of 200 desks. If vendor III is used, but fewer than 100 desks are purchased from vendor III, then a fixed ordering cost of $300 is incurred. The price of a desk is $495. The company has decided to order from not more than two vendors.

a. Formulate an ILP model and use the ILP program to find the solution.
b. If fewer than 80 desks are ordered from vendor III, then vendor I must be used. Add this constraint and resolve the problem.

7. A metropolitan health planning agency is trying to locate several Health Maintenance Clubs (HMCs) that provide prepaid health care. There are three potential site locations and fair communities to be served by these sites. The table below shows the number of subscribers that can be assigned to a site if an HMC is opened there. The ability to capture subscribers depends upon how close the site is to the community and its resident population. It is possible to locate HMCs at more than one site.

| | Community (000) | | | |
Site	1	2	3	4
1	50	10	25	20
2	20	15	20	40
3	25	20	10	25

Formulate a zero-one integer linear programming model to maximize total number of subscribers, using the variables

X_{ij} = 1 if subscribers from j is assigned to site i, 0 otherwise
Y_i = 1 if site i is selected for HMC, 0 otherwise

Assume the HMCs will satisfy the following conditions:

a. Each HMC will have a minimum enrollment of 50 (000) subscribers.
b. A community will be assigned to only one HMC.
c. If site 1 is selected, then either site 2 or site 3 may be selected, but not both.

Solve the problem by the ILP program.

8. A company manufactures gear boxes at three plants, and ships them to three company-owned distribution centers. The variable production and distribution costs per unit shipped between plants and distribution centers are given below. Also, the monthly production capacities of the plants, the monthly demand at the distribution centers, and the monthly fixed operating costs of plants and distribution centers are given.

Integer Linear Programming

	Plant	Distribution Center A	B	C	Monthly capacity	Fixed cost per month
Variable cost/unit	1	$25	$30	$27	600 units	$1700
	2	27	25	29	600	2000
	3	30	27	26	600	1900
Monthly demand		500	500 units	500		
Fixed cost per month		$500	$400	$600		

The company has been hit by a recession. Management has decided to close one plant and one distribution center. Of course, demand at the closed distribution center will be lost (not satisfied). When a distribution center is closed, nothing will be shipped to it, and the fixed operating costs will become negligible. When a plant is closed, nothing will be manufactured and shipped from it. However, one half of the monthly fixed operating costs of the closed plant will still be incurred.

a. Formulate an integer programming model to help in deciding which plant and distribution center to close. Solve the model by the ILP program.

b. Assume that management has decided to close either plant 1 or plant 3 if either distribution center A or B is closed. Add this constraint and solve the problem.

9. The WAC Corporation has been awarded a contract to produce 800 radar units. The delivery schedule is as follows:

$$\begin{array}{ll} \text{April 30} & \text{300 units} \\ \text{May 30} & \text{500 units} \end{array}$$

Deviations from this schedule are not permitted. Also, radar units produced in April for delivery on May 30 can be stored in WAC's warehouse at a cost of $15 per unit. Each radar unit requires 20 hours of assembly labor. On April 1, the start of the contract, WAC has a total of 80 trained workers on their payroll. In addition, new workers can be hired on April 1 or May 1, as necessary. Each trained worker produces 120 regular hours of assembly labor per month. Each new worker requires 30 hours of initial training and will, therefore, produce only 90 hours during his first month of employment and 120 hours during the subsequent months. All workers receive fixed wages of $1200 per month. All workers may be required to do overtime. However, the maximum overtime is restricted to 25 hours per month for any individual. Overtime is paid in addition to wages at $20 per hour. The cost of hiring new workers is $150 per worker and all hiring is done on the first of a month. WAC wishes to restrict their entire workforce to a maximum of 100 workers at any time. Further, it is WAC's policy not to lay off any worker. Assuming that exactly two trained workers will leave the company at the end of each month, WAC wishes to determine a minimum cost manpower plan for this contract.

Chapter 6
TRANSPORTATION PROBLEMS (TRP)

Overview of the TRP Decision Support System

This program solves transportation problems with up to 50 sources and 50 destinations. The capacities of the sources and the demands of the destinations are assumed to be integer; the cost/profit coefficients are assumed to be real valued. TRP provides an easy format to enter/modify the input data. Also, problems can be saved on or read from a disk(ette).

For small problems with up to four sources and five destinations, you have the option of displaying every iteration of the MOdified DIstribution (MODI) method. However, your TRP program can solve much larger problems. Also, you can select either Vogel's Approximation Method (VAM) or the NorthWest Corner method (NWC) for the initial feasible solution. After the problem has been solved, you can display and print the final solution.

The TRP decision support system allows you to define names of sources and destinations with up to six characters. The default names are S1, ..., Sn and D1, ..., Dn. Any time you want a copy of the output on the screen, press the F8 key.

Special Notes on the TRP Program

1. When entering a problem, use the BACKSPACE key to move the cursor to the position where you want to make corrections.

2. The TRP program uses the MOdified DIstribution (MODI) method (or Transportation Simplex method) to solve transportation problems with up to 50 sources and 50 destinations (including dummy sources and destinations). When total demand is not equal to total supply, the program will automatically add a dummy supply or demand.

3. When displaying the transportation tableau during the solution process, the stepping-stone path will be highlighted and the incoming basis (recipient cell) will be marked by "**".

4. Degeneracy is handled by a basis with 0 value.

5. If your problem data differ greatly (e.g., 0.0001 and 10000), you should normalize these data.

6. If there are big M values in your problem, you should enter large values that are much greater than any other data.

7. The TRP can read a file previously saved in the ASMP program, assuming that the supply and demand capacities are equal to 1.

Solving Problems with TRP

When you first select TRP, the function menu, shown in Fig. 6.1, will appear. You can now select the appropriate option.

```
Welcome to your Transportation Problem (TRP)  Decision Support System!
           The options available for TRP are as follows.
   If you are a first-time user, you might benefit from option 1.

      Option                  Function

         1      ----    Overview of TRP Decision Support System
         2      ----    Enter new problem
         3      ----    Read existing problem from disk(ette)
         4      ----    Display and/or print input data
         5      ----    Solve problem
         6      ----    Save problem on disk(ette)
         7      ----    Modify problem
         8      ----    Display and/or print final solution
         9      ----    Return to the program menu
         0      ----    Exit from QSB
```

FIGURE 6.1. Function menu of the TRP program.

The steps for using TRP to solve a transportation problem are listed below:

1. Analyze the problem: define sources and destinations and their capacities.

2. Formulate the transportation tableau.

3. Enter the problem into QSB (use option 2) or read the existing problem from a data disk(ette) (use option 3).

4. Display or print the problem if you want to check and verify data (use option 4).

5. Modify the problem as necessary (use option 7).

6. Solve the problem by displaying or without displaying steps (use option 5).

7. Display and print the final solution (use option 8).

8. Save the problem on a data disk(ette) if you may need it again (use option 6).

9. If you want to solve other problems, go to step 3. Otherwise, return to the program menu (use option 9) to select another program or exit from QSB (use option 0).

Example

To demonstrate the use of TRP, consider the following example problem. ABC Oil Company has three oil storage and four oil demand points. The company needs a shipping schedule that minimizes the total transportation cost and does not exceed the storage capacities. The demands and supplies and cost information are shown in Table 6.1. What is the best schedule to distribute oil from storage to demand points while minimizing the total transportation cost?

Table 6.1. Capacities and unit costs for ABC Company

		Demand point				
		Dallas	**Kansas**	**Tampa**	**Miami**	**Supply capacity**
	Boston	5	4	5	6	100
Storage	Denver	3	3	6	6	200
	Austin	2	5	7	8	400
	Demand	200	100	150	250	

Steps 1 and 2. Formulate the transportation tableau.

		Demand				
		Dallas	**Kansas**	**Tampa**	**Miami**	**Supply**
	Boston	5	4	5	6	100
Supply	Denver	3	3	6	6	200
	Austin	2	5	7	8	400
	Demand	200	100	150	250	

Step 3. Enter the problem (the data underlined in the following figures will be entered into TRP):

3.1. Enter problem name ABC.

3.2. Enter the information shown in Fig. 6.2 to define the problem. Note the conventions that appear on the screen when you enter data.

Transportation Problems

```
                    TRP Model Entry for ABC

Please observe the following conventions when entering a problem:

(1) Respond to the questions which seek general information about the problem.
(2) Then enter the names of sources and destinations, unless using defaults.
(3) Then enter the supplies, demands, and cost/profit coefficients.
(4) After you enter your data, press the ENTER key.
(5) On the same screen page, you may correct errors by pressing
    the BACKSPACE key to move the cursor to the correct position.
(6) When you are satisfied with the data on a page, press the SPACE BAR.
(7) When entering a problem, press the Esc key to go to the previous page;
    press the / key to go to the next page.

Do you want to maximize (1) or minimize (2) criterion? (Enter 1 or 2)<2 >

How many sources are there in your problem? (Enter number ≤ 50 )     <3 >

How many destinations are there in your problem? (Enter number ≤ 50 )<4 >

Do you want to use the default names (S1,...,Sn; D1,...,Dn)(Y/N)?     <n >
```

FIGURE 6.2. Screen display of TRP for defining a problem.

3.3. Figure 6.3 displays the screen for defining the names of sources and destinations. Note that we could use default names. After entering all names, press the SPACE BAR.

```
      Enter the Names of Sources and Destinations using at most 6 characters
 (To use default names, i.e., S1, . . ., Sn; D1, . . ., Dn, press the ENTER key)
Sources:
     1: <Boston> 2: <Denver> 3: <Austin>

Destinations:
     1: <Dallas> 2: <Kansas> 3: <Tampa > 4: <Miami >
```

FIGURE 6.3. Screen display for defining the names of sources and destinations.

3.4. Figure 6.4 displays the screen for entering the capacities of supplies and demands.

```
        Enter the Capacities of Sources and the Demands of Destinations
Sources:
   Boston:100___   Denver:200___   Austin:400___
Destinations:
   Dallas:200___   Kansas:100___   Tampa: 150___   Miami: 250___
```

FIGURE 6.4. Screen display for entering supplies and demands.

3.5. Figure 6.5 displays the screen for entering the cost or profit coefficient of each unit shipment. After entering each coefficient, press the ENTER key.

CHAPTER 6

```
              Enter the Cost/Profit Coefficients of the TRP Model
From     To
Boston   Dallas:5_____  Kansas:4_____  Tampa: 5_____  Miami: 6_____
Denver   Dallas:3_____  Kansas:3_____  Tampa: 6_____  Miami: 6_____
Austin   Dallas:2_____  Kansas:5_____  Tampa: 7_____  Miami: 8_____
```

FIGURE 6.5. Screen display for entering cost/profit coefficients.

Step 4. You may display the problem, as shown in Figs. 6.6 and 6.7.

```
           Input Data Describing Your Problem ABC (Capacities and Demands)
Sources:
   Boston:     100   Denver:    200   Austin:    400
Destinations:
   Dallas:     200   Kansas:    100   Tampa:     150   Miami:   250
```

FIGURE 6.6. Screen display of the supplies and demands for ABC.

```
           Input Data Describing Your Problem ABC (Cost/Profit Coefficients)
From     To
Boston   Dallas: 5.000  Kansas: 4.000  Tampa:  5.000 Miami:  6.000
Denver   Dallas: 3.000  Kansas: 3.000  Tampa:  6.000 Miami:  6.000
Austin   Dallas: 2.000  Kansas: 5.000  Tampa:  7.000 Miami:  8.000
```

FIGURE 6.7. Screen display of the cost/profit coefficients for ABC.

Step 5. You have the option of modifying the problem as needed. This gives the menu displayed in Fig. 6.8.

```
+----------------------------------------------------------------+
|                    Option Menu for Modifying ABC               |
+----------------------------------------------------------------+
|    Option                                                      |
|                                                                |
|       1    ----    Modify the capacity of sources/destinations |
|       2    ----    Add one source                              |
|       3    ----    Delete one source                           |
|       4    ----    Add one destination                         |
|       5    ----    Delete one destination                      |
|       6    ----    Modify the cost/profit coefficients         |
|       7    ----    Display and/or print input data             |
|       8    ----    Return to the function menu                 |
|                                                                |
+----------------------------------------------------------------+
```

FIGURE 6.8. Option menu for modifying a transportation problem.

Step 6. You are now ready to solve the problem. Select option 5 from the function menu. This will call up the solution menu shown in Fig. 6.9. Note that if you select an option from the solution menu, you will see every iteration on the screen. These iterations are shown in Figs. 6.10 to 6.14.

Transportation Problems

```
                   Option Menu for Solving ABC
    When solving a problem, you can display every iteration of the
MODI method if your problem scale is M < 5 and N < 6, where M is the
number of sources, N is the number of destinations.  Also you can use
the NorthWest Corner Method (NWC) or Vogel's Approximation Method
(VAM) to find the initial solution.  Default method is NWC.

        Option
            1   ----   Solve and display the initial tableau
            2   ----   Solve and display each iteration
            3   ----   Solve and display the final tableau
            4   ----   Solve without displaying any iteration
            5   ----   Use VAM for the initial solution
            6   ----   Return to the function menu
```

FIGURE 6.9. Option menu for solving ABC.

Initial solution by NWC

SN \ DN	Dallas	Kansas	Tampa	Miami	Supplies	U(i)
Boston	5.000 100.0	4.000	5.000	6.000	100.0	0
Denver	3.000 100.0	3.000 100.0	6.000 0	6.000	200.0	0
Austin	2.000	5.000	7.000 150.0	8.000 250.0	400.0	0
Demands V(j)	200.0 0	100.0 0	150.0 0	250.0 0		

Minimum Value of OBJ = 4150

FIGURE 6.10. The initial solution by NWC for the ABC problem.

Iteration 1

SN \ DN	Dallas	Kansas	Tampa	Miami	Supplies	U(i)
Boston	5.000 100.0	4.000	5.000 **	6.000	100.0	0
Denver	3.000 100.0	3.000 100.0	6.000 0	6.000	200.0	-2.000
Austin	2.000	5.000	7.000 150.0	8.000 250.0	400.0	-1.000
Demands V(j)	200.0 5.000	100.0 5.000	150.0 8.000	250.0 9.000		

Current Minimum Value of OBJ = 4150 with e(1, 3) =-3

FIGURE 6.11. The first iteration for the ABC problem.

CHAPTER 6

Iteration 2

SN \ DN	Dallas	Kansas	Tampa	Miami	Supplies	U(i)
Boston	5.000 100.0	4.000 0	5.000	6.000	100.0	0
Denver	3.000 100.0	3.000 100.0	6.000	6.000	200.0	-2.000
Austin	2.000 **	5.000	7.000 150.0	8.000 250.0	400.0	2.000
Demands V(j)	200.0 5.000	100.0 5.000	150.0 5.000	250.0 6.000		

Current Minimum Value of OBJ =   4150 with e(3, 1) =-5

FIGURE 6.12. The second iteration for the ABC problem.

Iteration 3

SN \ DN	Dallas	Kansas	Tampa	Miami	Supplies	U(i)
Boston	5.000	4.000	5.000 100.0	6.000	100.0	0
Denver	3.000 100.0	3.000 100.0	6.000	6.000 **	200.0	3.000
Austin	2.000 100.0	5.000	7.000 50.00	8.000 250.0	400.0	2.000
Demands V(j)	200.0 0	100.0 0	150.0 5.000	250.0 6.000		

Current Minimum Value of OBJ =   3650 with e(2, 4) =-3

FIGURE 6.13. The third iteration for the ABC problem.

Final tableau (Total iterations = 3)

SN \ DN	Dallas	Kansas	Tampa	Miami	Supplies	U(i)
Boston	5.000	4.000	5.000 100.0	6.000	100.0	0
Denver	3.000	3.000 100.0	6.000	6.000 100.0	200.0	0
Austin	2.000 200.0	5.000	7.000 50.00	8.000 150.0	400.0	2.000
Demands V(j)	200.0 0	100.0 3.000	150.0 5.000	250.0 6.000		

Minimum Value of OBJ =   3350 with multiple optimals.

FIGURE 6.14. The final iteration for the ABC problem.

Transportation Problems

Step 7. After the problem has been solved, you may use option 8 in the function menu to display or print the final solution. The menu of options available for displaying or printing is shown in Fig. 6.15. If you choose option 2 from this menu, then the final solution is displayed and automatically printed, as shown in Fig. 6.16.

```
Option Menu for Displaying and/or Printing the Final Solution to ABC
       You have the following options available for displaying
     or printing the final solution.  If you want to print the
     solution, make sure that the printer is ready.

     Option

         1   ----  Display the final solution only
         2   ----  Display and print the final solution
         3   ----  Return to the function menu
```

FIGURE 6.15. Option menu for displaying and printing solution.

```
                    Summary of Results for ABC      Page : 1

 From   To        Shipment  Unit cost  From    To       Shipment  Unit cost

 Boston Dallas       0.0      5.000    Denver  Tampa       0.0      6.000
 Boston Kansas       0.0      4.000    Denver  Miami     100.0      6.000
 Boston Tampa      100.0      5.000    Austin  Dallas    200.0      2.000
 Boston Miami        0.0      6.000    Austin  Kansas      0.0      5.000
 Denver Dallas       0.0      3.000    Austin  Tampa      50.0      7.000
 Denver Kansas     100.0      3.000    Austin  Miami     150.0      8.000

         Minimum value of OBJ =   3350 (multiple sols.)   Iterations = 3
```

FIGURE 6.16. The final solution for the ABC transportation problem.

Step 8. By choosing option 6 from the function menu, you can save the problem on a data disk(ette). Make sure that your data disk(ette) is formatted and inserted in the disk(ette) drive. Figure 6.17 gives the screen display for saving the problem.

```
                    Save Problem on Disk(ette)

         Decide on a file name for saving your problem.
         The file name may be the same as the problem name.
    Type x:xxxxxxxx.xxx for your file name ( e.g., A:XYZ.DAT ).

 What is your file name (Type A:, B:, or C: to see all the files) ? a:ABC.dat
```

FIGURE 6.17. Screen display for saving a problem.

Finding an Initial Solution—Vogel's Approximation Method (VAM)

When solving a transportation problem, Vogel's Approximation Method (VAM) may be used to find an initial solution. For the ABC distribution problem, if you choose option 5 and then option 1 from the solution menu, the initial solution will be obtained by the VAM method. Figure 6.18 shows this initial solution, and Fig. 6.19 shows that the final solution is the same as this initial solution.

```
                Initial solution by VAM
SN \ DN  Dallas    Kansas    Tampa     Miami     Supplies  U(i)
         5.000     4.000     5.000     6.000
Boston                       100.0               100.0     100.0
         3.000     3.000     6.000     6.000
Denver             100.0               100.0     200.0     100.0
         2.000     5.000     7.000     8.000
Austin   200.0               50.00     150.0     400.0     200.0
Demands  200.0     100.0     150.0     250.0
V(j)     200.0     100.0     50.00     150.0

             Minimum Value of OBJ = 3350
```

FIGURE 6.18. The initial solution by VAM.

```
         Final tableau (Total iterations = 0) by VAM
SN \ DN  Dallas    Kansas    Tampa     Miami     Supplies  U(i)
         5.000     4.000     5.000     6.000
Boston                       100.0               100.0     0
         3.000     3.000     6.000     6.000
Denver             100.0               100.0     200.0     0
         2.000     5.000     7.000     8.000
Austin   200.0               50.00     150.0     400.0     2.000
Demands  200.0     100.0     150.0     250.0
V(j)     0         3.000     5.000     6.000

     Minimum Value of OBJ = 3350 with multiple optimals.
```

FIGURE 6.19. The final iteration after the VAM initial solution.

Exercises

1. Consider the transportation problem with the following unit costs and capacities. Find the optimal solution by using the TRP program.

Source	A	Destination B	C	Supply
1	5	1	6	200
2	8	4	3	350
3	7	9	5	170
Demand	220	300	200	

Transportation Problems

2. Consider a distribution problem for which the unit transportation costs, demands, and supplies are listed as below. Find the optimal solution. Compare the iteration numbers to solve the problem by using the NorthWest Corner method or the Vogel's method as the initial solution method.

Source	Austin	Columbus	Destination Dallas	Boston	Los Angeles	Supply
New York	100	50	90	30	130	30000
Chicago	90	30	70	50	110	20000
Pittsburgh	95	30	75	40	120	20000
Demand	10000	12000	15000	17000	25000	

3. Nine jobs are available for ten persons. According to the skill levels, each person will have different earnings per hour for different jobs. The following table shows these earnings per hour. Use the TRP program to find the best assignment in order to maximize total earnings per hour for the ten persons.

Job	1	2	3	4	Person 5	6	7	8	9	10
1	3	1	8	4	3	2	7	4	2	5
2	6	1	3	5	6	6	3	8	9	10
3	9	4	3	1	5	6	9	3	1	2
4	7	9	3	4	8	4	6	9	3	1
5	2	5	7	4	2	1	2	2	6	8
6	5	4	3	4	3	7	8	6	5	9
7	8	7	6	3	9	4	3	5	6	1
8	5	4	2	8	7	6	3	7	8	9
9	5	9	1	3	6	7	4	2	1	5

4. Diho Dairy has two farms to supply milk for three local supermarkets. Demands for each supermarket during a delivery period are 6000, 4000, and 3800 gallons, respectively. Diho's two farms have capacities to produce 8500 gallons and 6500 gallons of milk respectively per delivery period. The distances from each farm to each supermarket are listed in the table. The company needs to find a shipping schedule in order to minimize the total transportation cost. Assume that the unit transportation cost is proportional to the travel distance.

Farm	Kenwood	Supermarket Submatrix	King Vegetable	Supply
Happy	5 miles	10	7	8500
Jucy	13	5	11	6500
Demand	6000	4000	3800	

CHAPTER 6

5. A company presently operates four manufacturing plants that distribute a product to three warehouses. Currently, the capacity of the plants and the demands of the warehouses are stable. These are listed with the unit shipping costs in the following table. Find the optimal distribution plan for the company.

Plant	Warehouse A	Warehouse B	Warehouse C	Monthly capacity
1	20	19	21	12200
2	19	22	18	2800
3	20	20	20	2500
4	21	20	19	2200
Monthly demand	7300	3500	5600	

6. A company has a six-month demand for its product broken down per month as follows: 1000, 1200, 1500, 2000, 1800, and 1500 units. The company has two ways to produce its product: regular time and overtime. The unit costs for regular time and overtime production are $10 and $14, respectively. Regular time can produce 1000 units per month; overtime can produce 800 units per month. The company can also hold the demands and satisfy them in the following months by giving customers a $2 discount per unit per one month delay. Maximum delay allowed is two months. Extra production will be carried to the next month. Carrying cost for each finished product is $3 per month. Formulate a transportation problem to represent this production planning problem to minimize the total production cost while meeting the demands. Use the TRP program to solve it.

Chapter 7
ASSIGNMENT PROBLEMS (ASMP)

Overview of the ASMP Decision Support System

This program solves assignment problems with up to 60 objects and 60 tasks. For example, tasks may represent jobs, and the objects may indicate workers. The problem criteria can be minimized or maximized, depending on the cost/profit coefficients corresponding to each object and task assignment. The program provides an easy format to enter and modify input data. Also, the problem can be saved on or read from a disk(ette).

For small problems with up to nine objects and nine tasks, you have the option of displaying every iteration of the Hungarian method. ASMP can solve many larger problems but without displaying every iteration. After the problem has been solved, you can display and print the final solution.

The ASMP decision support system allows you to define names of objects and tasks with up to six characters. The default names are O1, O2, ..., On and T1, T2, ..., Tn. Any time you want a copy of the screen output, press the F8 key.

Special Notes on the ASMP Program

1. When entering a problem, use the BACKSPACE key to move the cursor to the position where you want to make corrections.

2. The ASMP program uses the Hungarian method to solve assignment problems that are assumed to make one-to-one assignments. If the number of objects and the number of tasks are not the same, ASMP will automatically add the appropriate number of dummy tasks or objects.

3. If the numbers of objects and tasks are less than or equal to 9, ASMP may display the Hungarian method tableau, where zeros are crossed by "←" or "^".

4. If the problem is to maximize the objective, ASMP will convert it to a minimization problem by finding the appropriate opportunity loss for each potential assignment.

5. The ASMP program can read a file previously saved in the TRP program and assume there is a one-to-one assignment.

CHAPTER 7

Solving Problems with ASMP

When you first select ASMP, the function menu, shown in Fig. 7.1, will appear. You can now select the appropriate option. The steps for using ASMP to solve an assignment problem are listed below:

```
Welcome to your Assignment Problem (ASMP) Decision Support System!
         The options available for ASMP are as follows.
  If you are a first-time user, you might benefit from option 1.

    Option                    Function

       1      ----    Overview of ASMP Decision Support System
       2      ----    Enter new problem
       3      ----    Read existing problem from disk(ette)
       4      ----    Display and/or print input data
       5      ----    Solve problem
       6      ----    Save problem on disk(ette)
       7      ----    Modify problem
       8      ----    Display and/or print final solution
       9      ----    Return to the program menu
       0      ----    Exit from QSB
```

FIGURE 7.1. Function menu of the ASMP program.

1. Analyze and formulate an assignment tableau (see Table 7.1 for sample formulation).

2. Enter the problem into QSB (use option 2) or read the existing problem from the data disk(ette) (use option 3).

3. Display or print the problem if you want to check and verify data (use option 4).

4. Modify the problem as necessary (use option 7).

5. Solve the problem by displaying or without displaying intermediate steps (use option 5).

6. Display and print the final solution (use option 8).

7. Save the problem on a data disk(ette) if you may need it again (use option 6).

8. If you want to solve other problems, go to step 3. Otherwise, return to the program menu (use option 9) to select another program or exit from QSB (use option 0).

Example

To demonstrate the use of ASMP, consider the following example problem. Austin Computer Service Company (ACSC) has four customers who require service for their computer facilities. The customers are designated A, B, C, and D, respectively.

Assignment Problems

ACSC has four technicians capable of providing these services. Because of the different specialties of these technicians, their service times vary according to the specific customer. These service times are shown in Table 7.1. The manager of ACSC wants to determine an assignment schedule that will minimize the total service time for the four customers.

Table 7.1. Service times (in hours) of each technician working on a specific customer's computer facilities

Technician	A	B	C	D
John	3	6	7	10
Peter	5	6	3	8
Toshi	2	8	4	16
Rudy	8	6	5	9

(Customer)

Step 1. Formulate the problem as follows:

Objective: To minimize total service time.

Object	A	B	C	D
John	3	6	7	10
Peter	5	6	3	8
Toshi	2	8	4	16
Rudy	8	6	5	9

(Task)

Step 2. Enter the problem (the data underlined in the following figures will be entered into ASMP):

2.1. Enter problem name ACSC.

2.2. Enter the information shown in Fig. 7.2 to define the problem. Note the conventions that appear on the screen when you enter data.

```
Please observe the following conventions when entering a problem:
   (1) Respond to the questions which seek general information about the problem.
   (2) Then enter object and task names if you don't use default values.
   (3) Then enter cost/profit coefficients for each potential assignment.
   (4) After you enter your data, press the ENTER key.
   (5) On the same screen page, you may correct errors by pressing
       the BACKSPACE key to move the cursor to the correct position.
   (6) When you are satisfied with the data on a page, press the SPACE BAR.
   (7) When entering the problem, press the Esc key to go to a previous page;
       press the / key to go to the next page.
```

FIGURE 7.2. Screen display of ASMP for defining a problem.

CHAPTER 7

```
Do you want to maximize (1) or minimize (2) criterion? (Enter 1 or 2)<2 >
How many objects are there in your problem? (Enter number ≤ 60 )      <4 >
How many tasks are there in your problem? (Enter number ≤ 60 )        <4 >
Do you want to use the default names (O1,...,On; T1,...,Tn)(Y/N)?     <n >
```

FIGURE 7.2 *(cont.)* Screen display of ASMP for defining a problem.

2.3. Figure 7.3 displays the screen for defining the names of objects and tasks. Note that we could use default names. After entering the names, press the SPACE BAR.

```
        Enter the names of the objects and tasks using at most 6 characters
   (To use the default names, i.e., O1,...,On and T1,...,Tn, press the ENTER key)
Objects:
    1: <John  > 2: <Peter > 3: <Toshi > 4: <Rudy  >
Tasks:
    1: <A     > 2: <B     > 3: <C     > 4: <D     >
```
FIGURE 7.3. Screen display for defining the names of objects and tasks.

2.4. Figure 7.4 displays the screen for entering the cost/profit coefficients of each object at each task. After entering each coefficient, press the ENTER key.

```
                    Enter the Cost/Profit Coefficients

Objects  Tasks
John     A:    3_____  B:   6_____  C:   7_____  D:   10____
Peter    A:    5_____  B:   6_____  C:   3_____  D:    8____
Toshi    A:    2_____  B:   8_____  C:   4_____  D:   16____
Rudy     A:    8_____  B:   6_____  C:   5_____  D:    9____
```

FIGURE 7.4. Screen display for entering cost/profit coefficients.

Step 3. You may display or print the problem, as shown in Fig. 7.5.

```
Objects  Tasks
John     A:    3.000 B:   6.000 C:   7.000 D:   10.00
Peter    A:    5.000 B:   6.000 C:   3.000 D:    8.000
Toshi    A:    2.000 B:   8.000 C:   4.000 D:   16.00
Rudy     A:    8.000 B:   6.000 C:   5.000 D:    9.000
```

FIGURE 7.5. Screen display of the ACSC problem.

Step 4. You have the option of modifying the problem as needed. This gives the menu displayed in Fig. 7.6.

Assignment Problems

```
            Option Menu for Modifying ACSC
    Option
       1    ----    Modify cost/profit coefficients
       2    ----    Add one object
       3    ----    Delete one object
       4    ----    Add one task
       5    ----    Delete one task
       6    ----    Display and/or print input data
       7    ----    Return to the function menu
```

FIGURE 7.6. Option menu for modifying an assignment problem.

Step 5. You are now ready to solve the problem. Select option 5 from the function menu. This will call up the solution menu displayed in Fig. 7.7. Note that if you select option 2 from the solution menu, you will see every iteration on the screen. These iterations are shown in Figs. 7.8 to 7.10.

```
            Option Menu for Solving ACSC
   When solving your problem, you have the option of displaying every
iteration of the Hungarian method as long as your problem has less
than 10 objects and 10 tasks.
The problem ACSC has 4 objects and 4 tasks.
    Option
       1    ----    Solve and display the initial tableau
       2    ----    Solve and display each tableau
       3    ----    Solve and display the final tableau
       4    ----    Solve without displaying any tableau
       5    ----    Return to the function menu
```

FIGURE 7.7. Option menu for solving an assignment problem.

Initial tableau

Ob\Tk	A	B	C	D	Cov.Ln
John	3.000	6.000	7.000	10.00	
Peter	5.000	6.000	3.000	8.000	
Toshi	2.000	8.000	4.000	16.00	
Rudy	8.000	6.000	5.000	9.000	
Cov.Ln					

FIGURE 7.8. The initial tableau of the ACSC problem.

CHAPTER 7

Iteration 1

Ob\Tk	A	B	C	D	Cov.Ln
John	0	2.000	4.000	3.000	
Peter	2.000	2.000	0	1.000	<--
Toshi	0	5.000	2.000	10.00	
Rudy	3.000	0	0	0	<--
Cov.Ln	^				

FIGURE 7.9. The first iteration of the ACSC problem.

Final tableau (Total iterations = 2)

Ob\Tk	A	B	C	D	Cov.Ln
John	0	0	2.000	1.000	
Peter	4.000	2.000	0	1.000	
Toshi	0	3.000	0	8.000	
Rudy	5.000	0	0	0	
Cov.Ln	^	^	^	^	

FIGURE 7.10. The final iteration of the ACSC problem.

Step 6. After the problem has been solved, you may use option 8 in the function menu to display or print the final solution. The menu of options available for displaying or printing is shown in Fig. 7.11. If you choose option 2 from this menu, the final solution is displayed and automatically printed, as shown in Fig. 7.12.

```
Option Menu for Displaying and/or Printing the Final Solution to ACSC
      You have the following options available for displaying
   or printing the final solution.  If you want to print the
   solution, make sure that the printer is ready.

         Option

            1   ----   Display the final solution only
            2   ----   Display and print the final solution
            3   ----   Return to the function menu
```

FIGURE 7.11. Option menu for displaying and printing assignment solution.

Assignment Problems

```
        Summary of Assignments for ACSC      Page : 1
 Object      Task    Cost/Prof.   Object    Task    Cost/Prof.
  John        B        6.000      Toshi      A        2.000
  Peter       C        3.000      Rudy       D        9.000
           Minimum value of OBJ =  20   Total iterations = 2
```

FIGURE 7.12. The final solution of the ACSC assignment problem.

Step 7. By choosing option 6 from the function menu, you can save the problem on a data disk(ette). Make sure that your data disk(ette) is formatted and inserted in the disk(ette) drive. Figure 7.13 gives the screen display for saving your problem.

```
           Decide on a file name for saving your problem.
           The file name may be the same as the problem name.
      Type x:xxxxxxxx.xxx for your file name ( e.g., A:XYZ.DAT ).
What is your file name (Type A:, B:, or C: to see all the files) ? a:ACSC.dat
```

FIGURE 7.13. Screen display for saving the ACSC problem.

Exercises

1. The following assignment table shows the costs of finishing three jobs by three different persons. Assume each person is allowed to take one job. Use the ASMP program to solve this problem and show each step of the Hungarian method.

		Job	
Worker	1	2	3
A	10	12	25
B	19	20	22
C	15	26	17

2. Solve the following unbalanced assignment problem. M represents a huge penalty to make the assignment. (*Hint:* Use a number that is much larger than any number in the table to represent M.) All the numbers in the table represent costs.

CHAPTER 7

			Object		
Tasks	A	B	C	D	E
1	11	19	M	19	20
2	38	M	15	14	10
3	23	17	21	M	M
4	31	37	28	35	46
5	27	43	23	18	M
6	15	21	33	17	28

3. Solve problem 3 in Chapter 6 using the ASMP program.

4. On Monday morning, Super Garage has five cars coming in for service. Each of the five mechanics can service any of the cars. The number of hours required for each mechanic to repair each car is summarized below. What is the minimum total time assignment?

			Mechanic		
Car	Tedy	Bill	Simpson	Malon	Smith
Old	6	5	4.5	5.5	6
Chev	4	3.5	5	4.5	3
Toyo	2	3.5	3.5	4	3
Maz	5	4.5	3.5	4	5
Cadi	4	6	5.5	4.5	6

5. An organization in the United Nations has five agricultural consultants to help undeveloped countries to increase their food supply. Many African countries have famine problems because of the bad weather. Each consultant could help different countries to increase their food supply in different levels. The expected food increases per capita from each consultant are listed below. Assume each country has about the same population. Recommend a consultant-country assignment in order to maximize the food supply increase.

			Country		
Consultant	A	B	C	D	E
1	12	15	13	14	17
2	11	17	14	16	19
3	14	15	11	18	18
4	15	13	12	17	16
5	13	15	12	15	14

6. A young father won a game and received seven different toys as prizes. He has five children, but he doesn't know how to allocate these toys. As a good neighbor you suggest that he use a management science method to solve his problem. After a short discussion, both of you agree that each child, because each is of a

different age, may have different satisfaction or utility levels for each toy. Also, the father considers that two of his young children could get the second toy. You remind him that if a child receives two toys, the utility of the second toy will be only 60 percent of the original utility level. The satisfaction or utility level for each child for each toy is shown below. Assume child 1 and 2 are the youngest. Formulate an assignment problem and use the ASMP program to find a solution that maximizes total satisfaction.

| | Child | | | | |
Toy	1	2	3	4	5
A	5	6	7	8	9
B	4	3	5	7	6
C	3	8	6	7	5
D	7	5	4	3	5
E	6	4	7	5	4
F	8	7	6	6	5
G	7	7	8	6	7

Chapter 8
NETWORK MODELING (NET)

Overview of the NET Decision Support System

This program contains three well-known pure network algorithms: the shortest route algorithm, the maximal flow algorithm, and the minimal spanning tree algorithm. NET requires a network to represent the problem. The shortest route algorithm finds the shortest route from a start node to any other node on the network; the maximal flow algorithm finds the maximum flow from a source node to a sink node; and the minimal spanning tree algorithm finds the minimum total length of branches that link all nodes.

NET enables you to solve network problems with up to 150 branches and up to 75 nodes. It assumes that you have a network with the nodes numbered sequentially beginning with 1. Input data can be entered and modified in an easy fashion. Also, the problem can be saved on or read from a disk(ette). The network input data are performed branch by branch. The data for each branch include the start node, end node, and the distance or input/output flow between these two nodes.

After the data have been entered, you may choose options to solve the problems and display the results. Press the F8 key to print the output on the screen.

Special Notes on the NET Program

1. When entering a problem, use the BACKSPACE key to move the cursor to the position where you want to make corrections.

2. The NET program is designed to solve three typical network problems: the shortest route problem, the maximal flow problem, and the minimal spanning tree problem.

3. The data entry has a format for entering each arc (branch). Each arc requires that its start node and end node and its distance or flow capacities be specified. Arcs may be entered in random order.

4. Nodes should be numbered from leftmost node and sequentially beginning with 1. Also, the number of the start node on any arc should be lower than the number of the end node on that arc.

Network Modeling

5. The NET program can display every solution step. The shortest route problem is solved by a labeling procedure; the maximal flow problem is solved by a feasible flow searching procedure; and the minimal spanning tree problem is solved by a direct connecting procedure.

Solving Problems with NET

When you first select NET, the function menu, shown in Fig. 8.1, will appear. You can now select the appropriate option. The steps for using NET to solve the three typical network problems are listed below:

```
     Welcome to your NETwork modeling (NET) Decision Support System!
             The options available for NET are as follows.
     If you are a first-time user, you might benefit from option 1.

      Option                  Function

        1         ----    Overview of NET Decision Support System
        2         ----    Enter new problem
        3         ----    Read existing problem from disk(ette)
        4         ----    Display and/or print input data
        5         ----    Solve problem
        6         ----    Save problem on disk(ette)
        7         ----    Modify problem
        8         ----    Display and/or print final solution
        9         ----    Return to the program menu
        0         ----    Exit from QSB
```

FIGURE 8.1. Function menu of the NET program.

1. Analyze the problem: draw a network and number each node appropriately.

2. Enter the problem into QSB (use option 2) or read the existing problem from a data disk(ette) (use option 3).

3. Display or print the problem if you want to check and verify data (use option 4).

4. Modify the problem as necessary (use option 7).

5. Solve the problem by displaying or without displaying steps (use option 5).

6. Display and print the final solution (use option 8).

7. Save the problem on a data disk(ette) if you may need it again (use option 6).

8. If you want to solve other problems, go to step 3. Otherwise, return to the program menu (use option 9) to select another program or exit from QSB (use option 0).

CHAPTER 8

Examples

To demonstrate the use of NET, consider the following example problems.

The Shortest Route Problem

A network is shown in Fig. 8.2. The numbers on the branches represent the distances between nodes. What is the shortest route from node 1 to node 10?

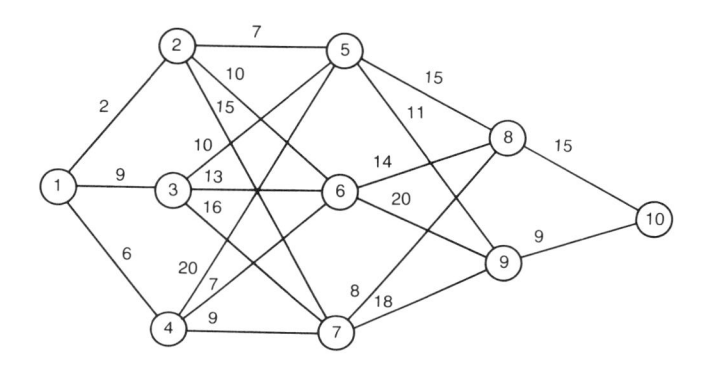

FIGURE 8.2. A network illustrating the shortest route.

Step 1. Prepare the network with appropriate numbered nodes, as shown in Fig. 8.2.

Step 2. Enter the problem (the data underlined in the following figures will be entered into NET):

2.1. Enter problem name and the numbers of branches and nodes, as shown in Fig. 8.3.

```
Please name your problem using up to 6 characters ? SRP
Your NET program can analyze networks with up to 150 branches and 75 nodes.
How many branches ( ≤ 150 ) are there in your problem SRP? 20
How many nodes ( ≤ 75 ) are there in your problem SRP? 10
```

FIGURE 8.3. Screen display for entering numbers of branches and nodes.

2.2. Select one of the three options in Fig. 8.4 to specify your problem. Note the conventions that appear on the screen before you enter data (Fig. 8.5).

Network Modeling

```
          Select one of the following algorithms:

              1 -- Shortest Route (Path) Algorithm
              2 -- Maximal Flow Algorithm
              3 -- Minimal Spanning Tree Algorithm
              4 -- Return to the function menu

          Enter your choice number ? 1
```

FIGURE 8.4. Screen display of NET for selecting problems.

```
                    NET Model Entry for SRP

Please observe the following conventions when entering a problem:

   (1) You may enter branch names up to 6 characters, defaults are B1,..,Bn.
   (2) Number each node sequentially beginning from 1 to  10 .
   (3) The sequence of branches is arbitrary in the following entry format.
   (4) After you enter your data, press the ENTER key.
   (5) On the same screen page, you may correct errors by pressing the
       BACKSPACE key to move the blinking cursor to the correct place.
   (6) When you are satisfied with the data on a page, press the SPACE BAR.
   (7) Press the Esc key to go to the previous page;
       press the / key to go to the next page.
```

FIGURE 8.5. Screen display for entry conventions.

2.3. Figure 8.6 displays the screen for entering each branch. Note that you can use default branch names (B1 to B20).

```
                       NET Model Entry for SRP Page 1

Branch      Branch        Start    End         Distance
Number      Name          Node     Node
  1       <       >       <1  >    <2  >       <2     >
  2       <       >       <1  >    <3  >       <9     >
  3       <       >       <1  >    <4  >       <6     >
  4       <       >       <2  >    <5  >       <7     >
  5       <       >       <2  >    <6  >       <10    >
  6       <       >       <2  >    <7  >       <15    >
  7       <       >       <3  >    <5  >       <10    >
  8       <       >       <3  >    <6  >       <13    >
  9       <       >       <3  >    <7  >       <16    >
 10       <       >       <4  >    <5  >       <20    >
 11       <       >       <4  >    <6  >       <7     >
 12       <       >       <4  >    <7  >       <9     >
 13       <       >       <5  >    <8  >       <15    >
 14       <       >       <5  >    <9  >       <11    >
 15       <       >       <6  >    <8  >       <14    >
 16       <       >       <6  >    <9  >       <20    >
 17       <       >       <7  >    <8  >       <8     >
 18       <       >       <7  >    <9  >       <18    >
 19       <       >       <8  >    <10 >       <15    >
 20       <       >       <9  >    <10 >       <9     >
```

FIGURE 8.6. Screen display for entering branches.

CHAPTER 8

Step 3. You may display or print the network data, as shown in Fig. 8.7.

```
                    Input Data Describing Your Problem SRP Page 1

Branch      Branch       Start      End        Distance
Number      Name         Node       Node
  1         <B1  >       <1  >      <2  >       <  2.00000>
  2         <B2  >       <1  >      <3  >       <  9.00000>
  3         <B3  >       <1  >      <4  >       <  6.00000>
  4         <B4  >       <2  >      <5  >       <  7.00000>
  5         <B5  >       <2  >      <6  >       < 10.00000>
  6         <B6  >       <2  >      <7  >       < 15.00000>
  7         <B7  >       <3  >      <5  >       < 10.00000>
  8         <B8  >       <3  >      <6  >       < 13.00000>
  9         <B9  >       <3  >      <7  >       < 16.00000>
 10         <B10 >       <4  >      <5  >       < 20.00000>
 11         <B11 >       <4  >      <6  >       <  7.00000>
 12         <B12 >       <4  >      <7  >       <  9.00000>
 13         <B13 >       <5  >      <8  >       < 15.00000>
 14         <B14 >       <5  >      <9  >       < 11.00000>
 15         <B15 >       <6  >      <8  >       < 14.00000>
 16         <B16 >       <6  >      <9  >       < 20.00000>
 17         <B17 >       <7  >      <8  >       <  8.00000>
 18         <B18 >       <7  >      <9  >       < 18.00000>
 19         <B19 >       <8  >      <10 >       < 15.00000>
 20         <B20 >       <9  >      <10 >       <  9.00000>
```

FIGURE 8.7. Screen display of the branch data.

Step 4. You have the option of modifying the data as needed. This gives the menu displayed in Fig. 8.8.

```
                    Option Menu for Modifying SRP
            Option
              1    ----   Modify branch data
              2    ----   Add one branch
              3    ----   Delete one branch
              4    ----   Change number of nodes
              5    ----   Exchange model criteria
              6    ----   Display and/or print input data
              7    ----   Return to the function menu
```

FIGURE 8.8. Option menu for modifying a problem.

Step 5. You are now ready to solve the problem. Select option 5 from the function menu. This will call up the solution menu, displayed in Fig. 8.9. Note that if you select option 1 from the solution menu, you will see every iteration on the screen. These iterations are shown in Fig. 8.10.

```
                    Option Menu for Solving SRP
      When solving a problem, you have the option of displaying each
   step of network algorithm.  Also you can choose to display or print
   the final solution.

                 Option

                    1    ----  Solve and display each step
                    2    ----  Solve without displaying steps
                    3    ----  Print the final solution
                    4    ----  Return to the function menu
```

FIGURE 8.9. Option menu for solving a NET problem.


```
Detailed Steps for the Shortest Route Algorithm:

Step 1 : Permanently label node  1
         Update the following nodes and labels (i.e., distance and from node):
             Node  2: ( 2 , 1 )
             Node  3: ( 9 , 1 )
             Node  4: ( 6 , 1 )

Step 2 : Permanently label node  2
         Update the following nodes and labels (i.e., distance and from node):
             Node  5: ( 9 , 2 )
             Node  6: ( 12 , 2 )
             Node  7: ( 17 , 2 )

Step 3 : Permanently label node  4
         Update the following nodes and labels (i.e., distance and from node):
             Node  7: ( 15 , 4 )

Step 4 : Permanently label node  3
         Update the following nodes and labels (i.e., distance and from node):
             None

Step 5 : Permanently label node  5
         Update the following nodes and labels (i.e., distance and from node):
             Node  8: ( 24 , 5 )
             Node  9: ( 20 , 5 )

Step 6 : Permanently label node  6
         Update the following nodes and labels (i.e., distance and from node):
             None

Step 7 : Permanently label node  7
         Update the following nodes and labels (i.e., distance and from node):
             Node  8: ( 23 , 7 )

Step 8 : Permanently label node  9
         Update the following nodes and labels (i.e., distance and from node):
             Node  10: ( 29 , 9 )

Step 9 : Permanently label node  8
         Update the following nodes and labels (i.e., distance and from node):
             None
Step 10 : Permanently label node  10
         Update the following nodes and labels (i.e., distance and from node):
             None
```

FIGURE 8.10. Screen display for shortest route solution steps.

CHAPTER 8

Step 6. After the problem has been solved, you may use option 8 in the function menu to display or print the final solution. The menu of options available for displaying or printing is shown in Fig. 8.11. If you choose option 2 from this menu, the final solution will be displayed and automatically printed as shown in Fig. 8.12.

```
Option Menu for Displaying and/or Printing the Final Solution to SRP
      You have the following options available for displaying
  or printing the final solution.  If you want to print the
  solution, make sure that the printer is ready.

         Option

            1   ----  Display the final solution only
            2   ----  Display and print the final solution
            3   ----  Return to the function menu
```

FIGURE 8.11. Screen display for displaying and printing solution.

```
              The Final Shortest Routes for SRP    Page: 1

Node    Distance     Shortest Route from Node 1

 2        2          1- 2  (B1)
 3        9          1- 3  (B2)
 4        6          1- 4  (B3)
 5        9          1- 2- 5  (B1-B4)
 6       12          1- 2- 6  (B1-B5)
 7       15          1- 4- 7  (B3-B12)
 8       23          1- 4- 7- 8  (B3-B12-B17)
 9       20          1- 2- 5- 9  (B1-B4-B14)
10       29          1- 2- 5- 9- 10  (B1-B4-B14-B20)
```

FIGURE 8.12. Screen display of the shortest route solution.

Step 7. By choosing option 6 from the function menu, you can save the problem on a data disk(ette). Make sure that your data disk(ette) is formatted and inserted in the disk(ette) drive. Figure 8.13 gives the screen display for saving a problem.

```
            Decide on a file name for saving your problem.
            The file name may be the same as the problem name.
        Type x:xxxxxxxx.xxx for your file name ( e.g., A:XYZ.DAT ).

What is your file name (Type A:, B:, or C: to see all the files) ? a:SRP.dat
```

FIGURE 8.13. Screen display for saving a problem.

A Minimal Spanning Tree

Suppose you want to find a tree that links all the nodes in Fig. 8.2 and minimizes the total distance of the tree. The procedure to enter the data for this problem is shown in Figs. 8.14 and 8.15, and the solution process displaying each step is shown in Figs. 8.16 and 8.17.

```
Please name your problem using up to 6 characters ? MSTREE

Your NET program can analyze networks with up to 150 branches and 75 nodes.

How many branches ( ≤ 150 ) are there in your problem MSTREE? 20

How many nodes ( ≤ 75 ) are there in your problem MSTREE? 10

Select one of the following algorithms:

    1 -- Shortest Route (Path) Algorithm
    2 -- Maximal Flow Algorithm
    3 -- Minimal Spanning Tree Algorithm
    4 -- Return to the function menu

Enter your choice number ? 3
```

FIGURE 8.14. Screen display for selecting minimal spanning tree.

```
                        NET Model Entry for MSTREE Page 1

   Branch    Branch      Start      End        Distance
   Number    Name        Node       Node
     1       <     >     <1  >      <2  >      <2  >
     2       <     >     <1  >      <3  >      <9  >
     3       <     >     <1  >      <4  >      <6  >
     4       <     >     <2  >      <5  >      <7  >
     5       <     >     <2  >      <6  >      <10 >
     6       <     >     <2  >      <7  >      <15 >
     7       <     >     <3  >      <5  >      <10 >
     8       <     >     <3  >      <6  >      <13 >
     9       <     >     <3  >      <7  >      <16 >
    10       <     >     <4  >      <5  >      <20 >
    11       <     >     <4  >      <6  >      <7  >
    12       <     >     <4  >      <7  >      <9  >
    13       <     >     <5  >      <8  >      <15 >
    14       <     >     <5  >      <9  >      <11 >
    15       <     >     <6  >      <8  >      <14 >
    16       <     >     <6  >      <9  >      <20 >
    17       <     >     <7  >      <8  >      <8  >
    18       <     >     <7  >      <9  >      <18 >
    19       <     >     <8  >      <10 >      <15 >
    20       <     >     <9  >      <10 >      <9  >
```

FIGURE 8.15. Screen display for entering branches.

The Maximal Flow Problem

A communications network, Fig. 8.18, transfers information among different locations. The numbers on each branch represent the information inflow and outflow capacities for that branch—for example, the flow capacity from node 1 to node 2 is 10, and that from node 2 to node 1 is 6. What is the possible maximum information flow from node 1 to node 7?

73

CHAPTER 8

```
Detailed Steps for the Minimal Spanning Tree Algorithm:

Step 1 : Connect node  1
         The unconnected node closest to the connected nodes is: Node 2
         The shortest distance is from node 1 to node 2 with distance 2

Step 2 : Connect node  2
         The unconnected node closest to the connected nodes is: Node 4
         The shortest distance is from node 1 to node 4 with distance 6

Step 3 : Connect node  4
         The unconnected node closest to the connected nodes is: Node 5
         The shortest distance is from node 2 to node 5 with distance 7

Step 4 : Connect node  5
         The unconnected node closest to the connected nodes is: Node 6
         The shortest distance is from node 4 to node 6 with distance 7

Step 5 : Connect node  6
         The unconnected node closest to the connected nodes is: Node 3
         The shortest distance is from node 1 to node 3 with distance 9

Step 6 : Connect node  3
         The unconnected node closest to the connected nodes is: Node 7
         The shortest distance is from node 4 to node 7 with distance 9

Step 7 : Connect node  7
         The unconnected node closest to the connected nodes is: Node 8
         The shortest distance is from node 7 to node 8 with distance 8

Step 8 : Connect node  8
         The unconnected node closest to the connected nodes is: Node 9
         The shortest distance is from node 5 to node 9 with distance 11

Step 9 : Connect node  9
         The unconnected node closest to the connected nodes is: Node 10
         The shortest distance is from node 9 to node 10 with distance 9

Step 10 : Connect node  10
         The unconnected node closest to the connected nodes is: None
```

FIGURE 8.16.   Screen display for minimal spanning tree solution steps.

```
            The Final Minimal Spanning Tree for MSTREE    Page: 1

            Branch on the Tree              Distance

                   1 -  2  (B1)                2
                   1 -  3  (B2)                9
                   1 -  4  (B3)                6
                   2 -  5  (B4)                7
                   4 -  6  (B11)               7
                   4 -  7  (B12)               9
                   5 -  9  (B14)              11
                   7 -  8  (B17)               8
                   9 - 10  (B20)               9

                   Total distance = 68
```

FIGURE 8.17.   Screen display of the minimal spanning tree.

Network Modeling

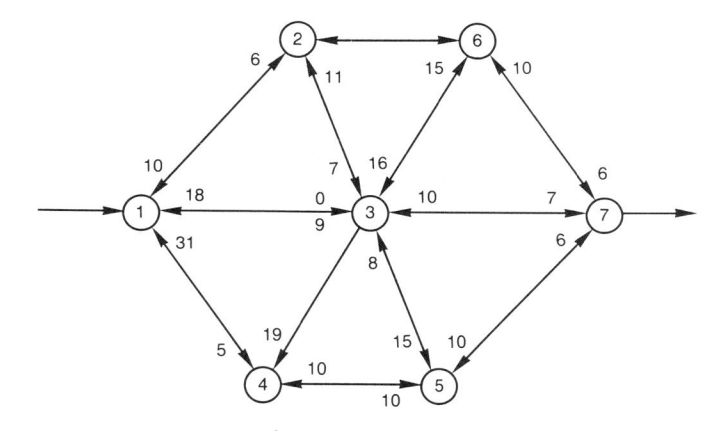

FIGURE 8.18. The network of a maximal flow problem.

To solve this problem using NET, the procedure to enter the data for this network is shown in Figs. 8.19 and 8.20, and the solution process is shown in Figs. 8.21 and 8.22.

```
Your NET program can analyze networks with up to 150 branches and 75 nodes.

How many branches ( ≤ 150 ) are there in your problem MFLOW? 12

How many nodes ( ≤ 75 ) are there in your problem MFLOW? 7


Select one of the following algorithms:

    1 -- Shortest Route (Path) Algorithm
    2 -- Maximal Flow Algorithm
    3 -- Minimal Spanning Tree Algorithm
    4 -- Return to the function menu

Enter your choice number ? 2
```

FIGURE 8.19. Screen display for selecting maximal flow.

```
                      NET Model Entry for MFLOW Page 1
   Branch      Branch      Start      End       Flow Capacity     Flow Capacity
   Number       Name        Node      Node     From Start Node   From End Node
      1       <       >    <1 >      <2 >         <10    >          <6   >
      2       <       >    <1 >      <3 >         <18    >          <0   >
      3       <       >    <1 >      <4 >         <31    >          <5   >
      4       <       >    <2 >      <6 >         <9     >          <20  >
      5       <       >    <2 >      <3 >         <11    >          <7   >
      6       <       >    <3 >      <4 >         <9     >          <19  >
      7       <       >    <3 >      <5 >         <8     >          <15  >
      8       <       >    <3 >      <6 >         <16    >          <15  >
      9       <       >    <3 >      <7 >         <10    >          <7   >
     10       <       >    <4 >      <5 >         <10    >          <10  >
     11       <       >    <5 >      <7 >         <10    >          <6   >
     12       <       >    <6 >      <7 >         <10    >          <6   >
```

FIGURE 8.20. Screen display for entering flow capacities.

CHAPTER 8

```
Detailed Steps for the Maximal Flow Algorithm:

Step 1 : Flow = 9, determined by branch   2 - 6
         The path selected is:   1- 2- 6- 7

Step 2 : Flow = 1, determined by branch   1 - 2
         The path selected is:   1- 2- 3- 4- 5- 7

Step 3 : Flow = 8, determined by branch   3 - 4
         The path selected is:   1- 3- 4- 5- 7

Step 4 : Flow = 1, determined by branch   5 - 7
         The path selected is:   1- 3- 5- 7

Step 5 : Flow = 1, determined by branch   6 - 7
         The path selected is:   1- 3- 6- 7

Step 6 : Flow = 8, determined by branch   1 - 3
         The path selected is:   1- 3- 7

Step 7 : Flow = 1, determined by branch   4 - 5
         The path selected is:   1- 4- 5- 3- 7

Step 8 : Flow = 1, determined by branch   3 - 7
         The path selected is:   1- 4- 3- 7
```

FIGURE 8.21. Screen display for maximal flow solution steps.

```
              The Final Flow for MFLOW    Page: 1

          Branch                      Net Flow

          1 - 2   (B1)                   10
          1 - 3   (B2)                   18
          1 - 4   (B3)                    2
          2 - 6   (B4)                    9
          2 - 3   (B5)                    1
          3 - 4   (B6)                    8
          3 - 6   (B8)                    1
          3 - 7   (B9)                   10
          4 - 5   (B10)                  10
          5 - 7   (B11)                  10
          6 - 7   (B12)                  10

              Maximal total flow = 30
```

FIGURE 8.22. Screen display for maximal flow.

Exercises

1. Find the shortest route from node 1 to 11 for the following network.

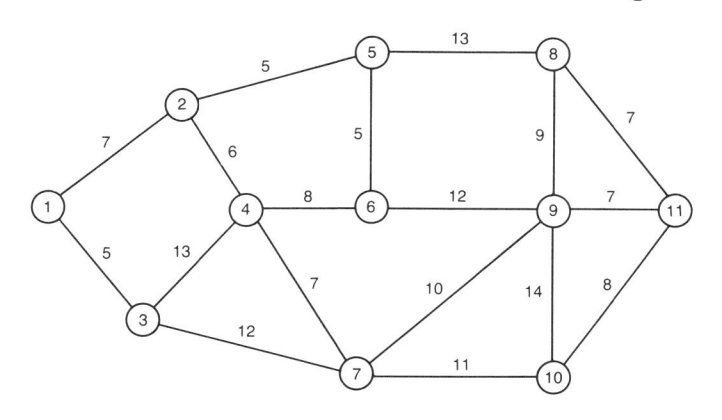

Network Modeling

2. Consider the network in problem 1. Find the minimal spanning tree.

3. Find the shortest routes from node 1 to every other node for the following network.

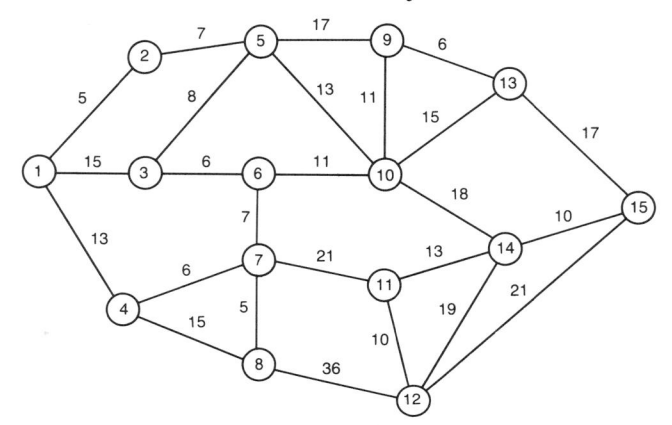

4. Consider the network in problem 3. Construct a minimal spanning tree.

5. The flow capacities between nodes are shown on the following network. Use the NET program to find the maximal flow from node 1 to node 11.

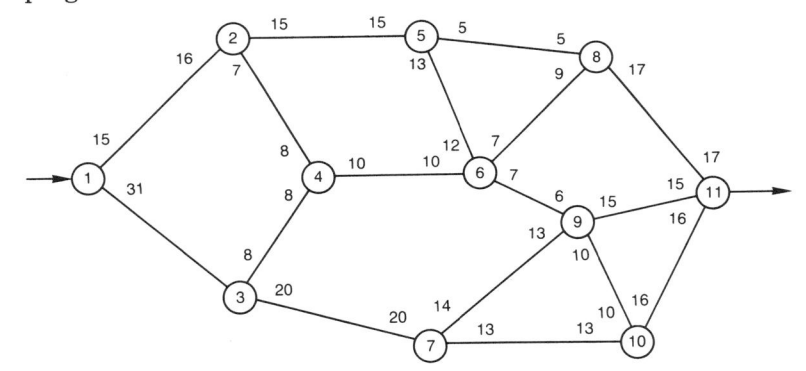

6. A new neighborhood is being built. The distances (in yards) between each house are summarized below. A local telephone company is trying to build a communications network for this neighborhood. How should the company connect the cable to minimize the total length?

| | | | | To house | | | |
From house	1	2	3	4	5	6	7
1	—	1500	1400	3500	3200	2500	3700
2	1500	—	4500	1700	2200	2300	2900
3	1400	4500	—	3100	2800	1900	1500
4	3500	1700	3100	—	1900	2500	2300
5	3200	2200	2800	1900	—	3500	1600
6	2500	2300	1900	2500	3500	—	5600
7	3700	2900	1500	2300	1600	5600	—

77

Chapter 9
CRITICAL PATH METHOD (CPM)

Overview of the CPM Decision Support System

This program analyzes project networks with up to 200 activities using the Critical Path Method (CPM). Each activity is assumed to have a deterministic duration and cost. You can perform "crash" analysis by entering crash times and costs. The program provides an easy format to enter and modify data. Also, the problem data can be saved on or read from a disk(ette). CPM assumes that each network uses an activity-on-arc format.

After a project has been analyzed, you can choose to display earliest start time (ES), latest start time (LS), earliest finish time (EF), and latest finish time (LF), as well as the slack and critical status of each activity. Also, your CPM will display up to ten critical paths of the network if the project has multiple critical paths.

The CPM Decision Support System allows you to define activity names with up to six characters. The default names are A1, A2, . . ., An. Note that activities as well as nodes must be numbered sequentially beginning with 1 and following the precedence relationship of the activities. Press the F8 key to print the output on the screen.

Special Notes on the CPM Program

1. When entering a problem, use the BACKSPACE key to move the cursor to the position where you want to make corrections.

2. CPM assumes that your project network has an activity-on-arc (AOA) format. A network with the AON (activity-on-node) format can always be converted to an AOA format. You can change each node on the AON network to an arc and add dummy arcs (activities) when necessary to convert to the AOA network. Dummy arcs are generally used to keep precedence relationships.

3. The CPM program solves the network in the sequence of the numbered nodes. It is necessary to number the start node lower than the end node for each activity and number each node sequentially beginning from 1.

4. At most ten critical paths can be displayed if your project has multiple critical paths.

5. Crash times and costs are required if you want to perform "crash" analysis.

6. Crashing is performed individually for each critical path. Therefore, if your network has multiple critical paths, the crash results may be approximate.

7. The crash analysis is performed by one full-time unit at one iteration.

Solving Problems with CPM

When you first select CPM, the function menu, shown in Fig. 9.1, will appear. You can now select the appropriate option.

The steps for using CPM to solve a project network are listed below:

```
Welcome to your Critical Path Method (CPM) Project Scheduling System!
         The options available for CPM are as follows.
   If you are a first-time user, you might benefit from option 1.

    Option                    Function

       1         ----    Overview of CPM Decision Support System
       2         ----    Enter new problem
       3         ----    Read existing problem from disk(ette)
       4         ----    Display and/or print input data
       5         ----    Solve problem
       6         ----    Save problem on disk(ette)
       7         ----    Modify problem
       8         ----    Display and/or print final solution
       9         ----    Return to the program menu
       0         ----    Exit from QSB
```

FIGURE 9.1. Function menu of the CPM program.

1. Analyze the problem: define the relationships among activities.

2. Draw a CPM network with the AOA format and number each node sequentially beginning with 1.

3. Enter the problem into QSB (use option 2) or read the existing problem from a data disk(ette) (use option 3).

4. Display or print the problem if you want to check and verify data (use option 4).

5. Modify the problem as necessary (use option 7).

6. Solve the problem and perform crash analysis (use option 5).

7. Display and print the final solution (use option 8).

8. Save the problem on a data disk(ette) if you may need it again (use option 6).

9. If you want to solve other problems, go to step 3. Otherwise, return to the program menu (use option 9) to select another program or exit from QSB (use option 0).

CHAPTER 9

Example

To demonstrate the use of CPM, consider the following example project. A construction project has 12 activities. Table 9.1 shows the completion times in days and costs of activities. The predecessors of each activity are also shown in the table, as well as the crash times and crash costs of activities. What is the normal completion time and total cost for the entire project? What is the critical path? If management wants to speed up the project by two days, how can this be done?

Table 9.1. Times and costs for the construction project

Activity No.	Name	Normal time	Crash time	Normal cost	Crash cost	Predecessor
1	A	5	3	2000	2500	—
2	B	4	4	3000	3000	—
3	C	8	7	4000	5000	—
4	D	3	2	1200	1500	A
5	E	7	5	2000	3000	A
6	F	5	5	3000	3000	C
7	G	4	3	3000	3700	C
8	H	3	3	8000	8000	B,D
9	I	9	6	700	1600	F,H
10	J	11	7	1500	2000	F,H
11	K	8	6	600	1500	E,I
12	L	10	9	1000	1050	G,J

Steps 1 and 2: Analyze and draw the AOA network. Then number each node, as shown in Fig. 9.2.

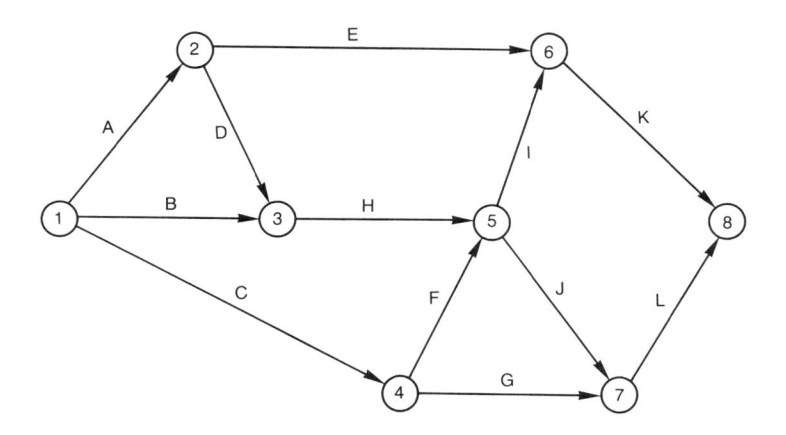

FIGURE 9.2. Network for the construction project.

Step 3. Enter the problem (the data underlined in the following figures will be entered into CPM):

3.1. Enter the problem name and the number of activities, as shown in Fig. 9.3.

```
Please name your problem using up to 6 characters ? CONSTR

Your CPM program can analyze projects with up to 200 activities.

How many activities are there in project CONSTR, including dummy activities? 12
```

FIGURE 9.3. Screen display for defining a project.

3.2. Enter each activity and its related times and costs, as shown in Fig. 9.4. (Note the conventions shown in Fig. 9.5.)

```
                       CPM Entry for CONSTR Page 1

Activity  Activity    Start     End      Normal     Crash     Normal       Crash
number      name      node      node    duration  duration    cost         cost
   1        <A  >     <1 >      <2 >     <5   >    <3  >     <2000 >     <2500 >
   2        <B  >     <1 >      <3 >     <4   >    <4  >     <3000 >     <3000 >
   3        <C  >     <1 >      <4 >     <8   >    <7  >     <4000 >     <5000 >
   4        <D  >     <2 >      <3 >     <3   >    <2  >     <1200 >     <1500 >
   5        <E  >     <2 >      <6 >     <7   >    <5  >     <2000 >     <3000 >
   6        <F  >     <4 >      <5 >     <5   >    <5  >     <3000 >     <3000 >
   7        <G  >     <4 >      <7 >     <4   >    <3  >     <3000 >     <3700 >
   8        <H  >     <3 >      <5 >     <3   >    <3  >     <8000 >     <8000 >
   9        <I  >     <5 >      <6 >     <9   >    <6  >     <700  >     <1600 >
  10        <J  >     <5 >      <7 >     <11  >    <7  >     <1500 >     <2000 >
  11        <K  >     <6 >      <8 >     <8   >    <6  >     <600  >     <1500 >
  12        <L  >     <7 >      <8 >     <10  >    <9  >     <1000 >     <1050 >
```

FIGURE 9.4. Screen display for entering activities.

```
                       CPM Entry for CONSTR

Please observe the following conventions when entering a problem:

   (1) Activity names can contain up to 6 characters.
   (2) Durations can contain up to 6 digits as well as a decimal point.
   (3) Costs can contain up to 6 digits as well as a decimal point.
   (4) If you do not have crash times and costs, leave these entries blank.
   (5) Start node number must be lower than an end node number.
   (6) After you enter your data, press the ENTER key.
   (7) On the same screen page, you may correct errors by pressing the
       BACKSPACE key to move the blinking cursor to the correct place.
   (8) When you are satisfied with the data on a page, press the SPACE BAR.
   (9) Press the Esc key to go to the previous page;
       press the / key to go to the next page.
```

FIGURE 9.5. Screen display for entry conventions.

Step 4. You may display or print the data, as shown in Fig. 9.6.

CHAPTER 9

```
              Input Data Describing Your Problem CONSTR Page 1
Activity  Activity     Start      End      Normal     Crash      Normal     Crash
 number    name        node       node    duration   duration     cost       cost
   1       <A   >      <1  >      <2  >   <5.0000>   <3.0000>   <2000.0>   <2500.0>
   2       <B   >      <1  >      <3  >   <4.0000>   <4.0000>   <3000.0>   <3000.0>
   3       <C   >      <1  >      <4  >   <8.0000>   <7.0000>   <4000.0>   <5000.0>
   4       <D   >      <2  >      <3  >   <3.0000>   <2.0000>   <1200.0>   <1500.0>
   5       <E   >      <2  >      <6  >   <7.0000>   <5.0000>   <2000.0>   <3000.0>
   6       <H   >      <3  >      <5  >   <3.0000>   <3.0000>   <8000.0>   <8000.0>
   7       <F   >      <4  >      <5  >   <5.0000>   <5.0000>   <3000.0>   <3000.0>
   8       <G   >      <4  >      <7  >   <4.0000>   <3.0000>   <3000.0>   <3700.0>
   9       <I   >      <5  >      <6  >   <9.0000>   <6.0000>   <700.00>   <1600.0>
  10       <J   >      <5  >      <7  >   <11.000>   <7.0000>   <1500.0>   <2000.0>
  11       <K   >      <6  >      <8  >   <8.0000>   <6.0000>   <600.00>   <1500.0>
  12       <L   >      <7  >      <8  >   <10.000>   <9.0000>   <1000.0>   <1050.0>
```

FIGURE 9.6. Screen display of each activity.

Step 5. You have the option of modifying the data as needed. This gives the menu displayed in Fig. 9.7.

```
            Option Menu for Modifying CONSTR
   Option

      1    ----    Modify duration/cost
      2    ----    Add one activity
      3    ----    Delete one activity
      4    ----    Display and/or print input data
      5    ----    Return to the function menu
```

FIGURE 9.7. Option menu for modifying a CPM problem.

Step 6. You are now ready to solve the problem. Select option 5 from the function menu. This will call up the solution menu displayed in Fig. 9.8. Note that if you select option 1 from the solution menu, you will see intermediate results on the screen. These are shown in Figs. 9.9 and 9.10. You may select option 4 from the solution menu and perform crash analysis to determine the effects of expediting the project, as illustrated in Fig. 9.11.

```
                Option Menu for Solving CONSTR
     When solving a problem, you have the option of displaying the
  intermediate results of the CPM method.  Also you can choose to
  perform 'crash' analysis if you have already entered the crash times
  and crash costs.  Your CPM program can display up to 10 critical
  paths if your project network has multiple critical paths.

     Option

        1    ----    Solve and display the intermediate results
        2    ----    Solve without displaying any result
        3    ----    Print the final solution
        4    ----    Perform crash analysis
        5    ----    Return to the function menu
```

FIGURE 9.8. Option menu for solving a CPM problem.

Critical Path Method

```
              CPM Analysis for CONSTR     Page  1
 Activity  Activity  Earliest   Latest    Earliest   Latest    Slack
 Number    Name      Start      Start     Finish     Finish    LS-ES

   1         A         0         2.0000    5.0000     7.0000    2.0000
   2         B         0         6.0000    4.0000    10.000     6.0000
   3         C         0         0         8.0000     8.0000    Critical
   4         D         5.0000    7.0000    8.0000    10.000     2.0000
   5         E         5.0000   19.000    12.000     26.000    14.000
   6         H         8.0000   10.000    11.000     13.000     2.0000
   7         F         8.0000    8.0000   13.000     13.000    Critical
   8         G         8.0000   20.000    12.000     24.000    12.000
   9         I        13.000    17.000    22.000     26.000     4.0000
  10         J        13.000    13.000    24.000     24.000    Critical
  11         K        22.000    26.000    30.000     34.000     4.0000
  12         L        24.000    24.000    34.000     34.000    Critical

              Completion time = 34    Total cost = 30000
```

FIGURE 9.9. CPM analysis for the construction project.

```
Critical paths for CONSTR  with completion time =  34   Total cost = 30000
CP # 1   :
            C            F            J            L
        1———————> 4———————> 5———————> 7———————> 8
```
FIGURE 9.10. Critical path.

```
                    Crash Analysis for CONSTR

    If you have not entered crash times and costs, please reply 'N' to
the following question.

Have you entered crash times and crash costs (Y/N)?Y

    The following crash analysis displays results step by step.  Of course,
the crash solution method is a heuristic and is likely to yield the optimal
solution all the time.  Before performing crash analysis, make sure you have
already saved the network on disk(ette) by using option 6 and print the
solution by using option 8 in the function menu.  The original data will be
destroyed while performing crash analysis.

Completion time for CONSTR is  34

Do you want to crash one time unit (Y/N)?

  For this crash:
    Crash activity: L  New duration:  9   Incremental cost:  50
Critical paths for CONSTR  with completion time =  33   Total cost = 30050
CP # 1   :
            C            F            J            L
        1———————> 4———————> 5———————> 7———————> 8
  For this crash:
    Crash activity: L  New duration:  9   Incremental cost:  50
Critical paths for CONSTR  with completion time =  33   Total cost = 30050
CP # 1   :
            C            F            J            L
        1———————> 4———————> 5———————> 7———————> 8
```

FIGURE 9.11. Crashing analysis.

CHAPTER 9

```
Do you want to crash one time unit (Y/N)?

  For this crash:
    Crash activity: J   New duration:  10   Incremental cost:  125
Critical paths for CONSTR  with completion time = 32   Total cost = 30175

CP # 1 :
     C               F             J             L
  1───────> 4───────> 5───────> 7───────> 8

Do you want to crash one time unit (Y/N)?
```

FIGURE 9.11 *(cont.)* Crashing analysis.

Step 7. After the problem has been solved, you may use option 8 in the function menu to display or print the final solution. The menu of options available for displaying or printing is shown in Fig. 9.12. If you choose option 2 from this menu, the final analysis and critical path are displayed and automatically printed, as shown in Figs. 9.13 and 9.14.

```
Option Menu for Displaying and/or Printing the Final Solution to CONSTR
        You have the following options available for displaying
     or printing the final solution.  If you want to print the
     solution, make sure that the printer is ready.

         Option

           1    ────   Display the final solution only
           2    ────   Display and print the final solution
           3    ────   Return to the function menu
```

FIGURE 9.12. Option menu for displaying and printing CPM solution.

```
                    CPM Analysis for CONSTR    Page  1
  Activity  Activity  Earliest   Latest    Earliest   Latest     Slack
  Number    Name      Start      Start     Finish     Finish     LS-ES

     1        A        0         2.0000     5.0000    7.0000     2.0000
     2        B        0         6.0000     4.0000   10.000      6.0000
     3        C        0         0          8.0000    8.0000     Critical
     4        D        5.0000    7.0000     8.0000   10.000      2.0000
     5        E        5.0000   17.000     12.000    24.000     12.000
     6        H        8.0000   10.000     11.000    13.000      2.0000
     7        F        8.0000    8.0000    13.000    13.000      Critical
     8        G        8.0000   19.000     12.000    23.000     11.000
     9        I       13.000    15.000     22.000    24.000      2.0000
    10        J       13.000    13.000     23.000    23.000      Critical
    11        K       22.000    24.000     30.000    32.000      2.0000
    12        L       23.000    23.000     32.000    32.000      Critical

              Completion time = 32    Total cost = 30175
```

FIGURE 9.13. CPM analysis.

Critical Path Method

```
Critical paths for CONSTR   with completion time =  32    Total cost = 30175
CP # 1  :
        C           F           J           L
    1-------> 4-------> 5-------> 7-------> 8
```

FIGURE 9.14. Critical path.

Step 8. By choosing option 6 from the function menu, you can save the problem on a data disk(ette). Make sure that your data disk(ette) is formatted and inserted in the disk(ette) drive. Figure 9.15 gives the screen display for saving this problem.

```
            Decide on a file name for saving your problem.
          The file name may be the same as the problem name.
        Type x:xxxxxxxx.xxx for your file name ( e.g., A:XYZ.DAT ).

What is your file name (Type A:, B:, or C: to see all the files) ? a:CONSTR.dat
```

FIGURE 9.15. Screen display for saving a problem.

Exercises

1. Consider the following project network with the AOA convention. Find the ES, LS, EF, LF, and criticality of each activity. Also find the critical path.

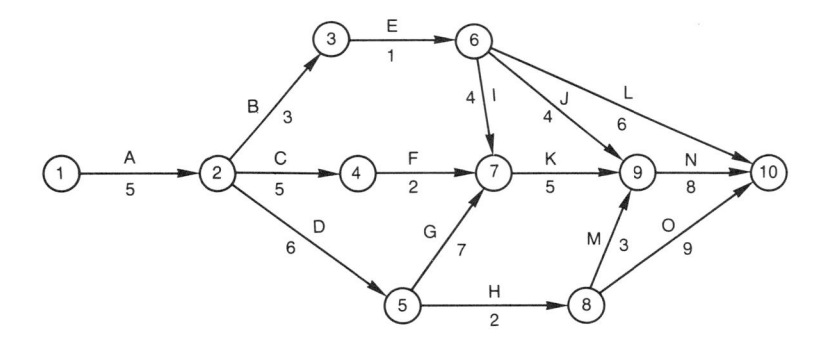

2. Perform the CPM analysis for the following AOA project network.

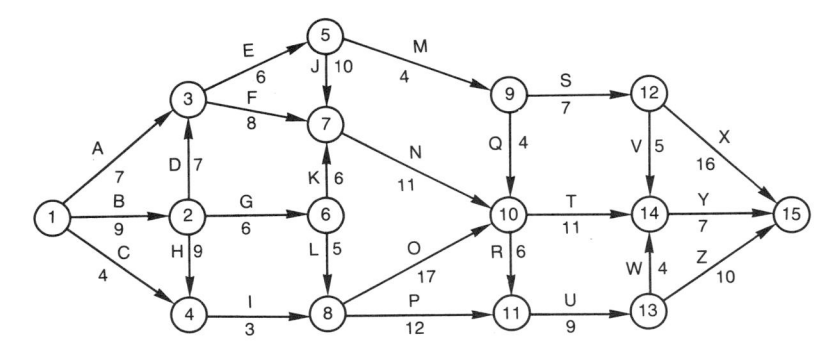

3. In planning a project to introduce a new product, the required activities are shown in the table.

Activity	Description	Immediate predecessor	Duration
A	Product design	—	5 months
B	Market research	—	1
C	Production analysis	A	2
D	Product model	A	3
E	Sales brochure	A	2
F	Cost analysis	C	3
G	Product testing	D	4
H	Sales training	B,E	2
I	Pricing and forecasting	H	1
J	Project report	F,G,I	1

  a. Construct a CPM network.
  b. Use the CPM program to find the critical path and its completion time.

4. The following information relates to the times and costs of activities in a project. The scheduled completion time is eight weeks. There is a $2500 per week penalty cost for each week delayed beyond the scheduled time. There also is a $1000 per week incentive bonus paid for each week ahead of schedule for the project completion. The activities listed in the table are associated with the AOA convention. For example, activity 1-2 represents nodes 1 to 2.

Activity	Normal time	Normal cost	Crash time	Crash cost
1-2	3 weeks	$3000	2 weeks	$5000
1-3	4	4000	2	6000
1-4	5	5000	3	8000
2-3	0	0	0	0
2-5	8	5000	6	6000
3-5	3	3000	2	4000
4-5	5	4000	3	8000

  a. Using normal times, determine the critical path.
  b. Determine the best (least cost) schedule for carrying out the project.

5. The information in the table relates to the activities necessary for completing a project.

Critical Path Method

Activity	Immediate predecessor	Normal time	Normal cost	Crash time	Crash cost
A	—	8 weeks	$4000	6 weeks	$ 6000
B	—	5	1500	4	2000
C	—	6	2500	4	3000
D	A	4	1800	3	2000
E	A,B	6	1000	5	1200
F	C	7	2000	5	3000
G	A	5	3000	3	6000
H	D,E,F	8	4500	5	9000
I	C	9	6000	4	10000
J	D,E,F	6	6000	4	8000
K	G,H	4	2000	3	3200
L	D,E,F	6	3000	3	9000
M	I,J	4	8000	2	12000

The schedule completion time of the project is 25 weeks. There is a $1500 penalty for each week the project is delayed beyond the scheduled completion time.
a. Construct an AOA network to represent this project.
b. Use the normal time to find the critical path and its completion time.
c. Determine the optimal (least cost) schedule for this project.

Chapter 10
PROGRAM EVALUATION AND REVIEW TECHNIQUE (PERT)

Overview of the PERT Decision Support System

This program analyzes project networks with up to 200 activities using the Program Evaluation and Review Technique (PERT). The activity durations are assumed to be beta distributed with three time estimates—optimistic, most likely, and pessimistic. The program provides an easy format to enter and modify data. Also, the problem data can be saved on or read from a disk(ette). PERT assumes that each network uses an activity-on-arc format.

After your project has been analyzed, you can choose to display earliest start (ES), latest start (LS), earliest finish (EF), and latest finish (LF) times, as well as the slack and critical status of each activity. Your PERT will display up to ten critical paths of the network if the project has multiple critical paths. You can also perform probability analysis.

The PERT decision support system allows you to define activity names with up to six characters. The default names are A1, A2, . . ., An. Note that activities as well as nodes must be numbered sequentially beginning with 1 and following the precedence relationship of the activities. Press the F8 key to print the output on the screen.

Special Notes on the PERT Program

1. When entering a problem, use the BACKSPACE key to move the cursor to the position where you want to make corrections.

2. PERT assumes that your project network has an activity-on-arc (AOA) format. A network with AON (activity-on-node) format always can be converted to an AOA network. The general way to convert an AON network to an AOA network is to change each node to an activity and add dummy arcs (activities) when necessary. Dummy arcs are generally used to keep precedence relationships.

3. The PERT program solves the network in the sequence of the numbered nodes. It is necessary to number the start node lower than the end node for each activity and number the nodes sequentially beginning with 1.

4. The completion time for each activity is assumed to be beta distributed with three time estimates.

5. At most ten critical paths can be displayed if your project has multiple critical paths.

6. When you perform the probability analysis, it is assumed that each critical path is independent and that the total completion time of each critical path is normal distributed. Therefore, if the critical paths are not independent or the number of activities on each critical path is not large enough, the results will tend to be biased.

Solving Problems with PERT

When you first select PERT, the function menu, shown in Fig. 10.1, will appear. You can now select the appropriate option. The steps for using PERT to solve a project network are listed below:

```
              Welcome to your PERT Project Scheduling System!
                The options available for PERT are as follows.
     If you are a first-time user, you might benefit from option 1.

       Option                    Function

         1        ----    Overview of PERT Decision Support System
         2        ----    Enter new problem
         3        ----    Read existing problem from disk(ette)
         4        ----    Display and/or print input data
         5        ----    Solve problem
         6        ----    Save problem on disk(ette)
         7        ----    Modify problem
         8        ----    Display and/or print final solution
         9        ----    Return to the program menu
         0        ----    Exit from QSB
```

FIGURE 10.1. Function menu of the PERT program.

1. Analyze the problem: define the relationships among activities.

2. Draw a PERT network with AOA format and number nodes sequentially beginning from 1.

3. Enter the problem into QSB (use option 2) or read the existing problem from a data disk(ette) (use option 3).

4. Display or print the problem if you want to check and verify data (use option 4).

5. Modify the problem as necessary (use option 7).

6. Solve the problem and perform probability analysis (use option 5).

7. Display and print the final solution (use option 8).

8. Save the problem on a data disk(ette) if you may need it again (use option 6).

9. If you want to solve other problems, go to step 3. Otherwise, return to the program menu (use option 9) to select another program or exit from QSB (use option 0).

CHAPTER 10

Example

The use of PERT is illustrated with the following example. Consider the construction project shown in Table 10.1. The optimistic times occur when everything goes smoothly, the most likely times occur in a normal situation, and the pessimistic times occur when the weather gets very bad. Management wants to know the expected completion time of the entire project and its critical path. Management also wants to estimate the probability of finishing the project within 30 days, 33 days, and 35 days.

Table 10.1. Three time estimates (in days) for the construction project

Activity No.	Name	Optimistic time	Most likely time	Pessimistic time	Predecessor
1	A	3	5	7	—
2	B	4	4	5	—
3	C	5	8	10	—
4	D	2	3	4	A
5	E	5	7	9	A
6	F	4	5	6	C
7	G	3	4	8	C
8	H	3	3	3	B,D
9	I	9	9	12	F,H
10	J	10	11	12	F,H
11	K	6	8	11	E,I
12	L	8	10	12	G,J

Steps 1 and 2: Analyze and draw the AOA network. Then number each node, as shown in Fig. 10.2.

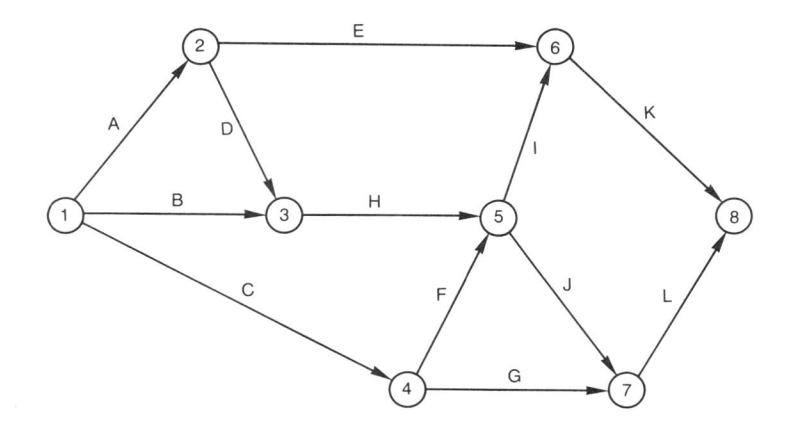

FIGURE 10.2. Network for the construction project.

Program Evaluation and Review Technique

Step 3. Enter the problem (the data underlined in the following figures will be entered into PERT):

3.1. Enter problem name and number of activities, as shown in Fig. 10.3.

```
Please name your problem using up to 6 characters ? CONSTR
Your PERT program can analyze projects with up to 200 activities.
How many activities are there in project CONSTR, including dummy activities? 12
```
FIGURE 10.3. Screen display for defining a project.

3.2. Enter each activity and its three time estimates, as shown in Fig. 10.4. Note the conventions shown in Fig. 10.5.

```
                         PERT Entry for CONSTR Page 1

Activity   Activity       Start      End       Optimistic     Most likely    Pessimistic
 number      name         node       node         Time           Time           Time
    1        <A    >      <1  >      <2  >       <3    >        <5    >        <7    >
    2        <B    >      <1  >      <3  >       <4    >        <4    >        <5    >
    3        <C    >      <1  >      <4  >       <5    >        <8    >        <10   >
    4        <D    >      <2  >      <3  >       <2    >        <3    >        <4    >
    5        <E    >      <2  >      <6  >       <5    >        <7    >        <9    >
    6        <F    >      <4  >      <5  >       <4    >        <5    >        <6    >
    7        <G    >      <4  >      <7  >       <3    >        <4    >        <8    >
    8        <H    >      <3  >      <5  >       <3    >        <3    >        <3    >
    9        <I    >      <5  >      <6  >       <7    >        <9    >        <12   >
   10        <J    >      <5  >      <7  >       <10   >        <11   >        <12   >
   11        <K    >      <6  >      <8  >       <6    >        <8    >        <11   >
   12        <L    >      <7  >      <8  >       <8    >        <10   >        <12   >
```
FIGURE 10.4. Screen display for entering activities.

```
                         PERT Entry for CONSTR

Please observe the following conventions when entering a problem:
    (1) Activity names can contain up to 6 characters.
    (2) Durations can contain up to 6 digits as well as a decimal.
    (3) Start node number must be lower than an end node number.
    (4) After you enter your data, press the ENTER key.
    (5) On the same screen page, you may correct errors by pressing the
        BACKSPACE key to move the blinking cursor to the correct place.
    (6) When you are satisfied with the data on a page, press the SPACE BAR.
    (7) Press the Esc key to go to the previous page;
        press the / key to go to the next page.
```
FIGURE 10.5. Screen display for entry conventions.

Step 4. You may display or print the data, as shown in Fig. 10.6.

CHAPTER 10

```
                    Input Data Describing Your Problem CONSTR Page 1
Activity   Activity     Start      End       Optimistic     Most likely    Pessimistic
 number     name        node       node         Time           Time           Time
    1       <A >        <1 >       <2 >       <3.0000>       <5.0000>       <7.0000>
    2       <B >        <1 >       <3 >       <4.0000>       <4.0000>       <5.0000>
    3       <C >        <1 >       <4 >       <5.0000>       <8.0000>       <10.000>
    4       <D >        <2 >       <3 >       <2.0000>       <3.0000>       <4.0000>
    5       <E >        <2 >       <6 >       <5.0000>       <7.0000>       <9.0000>
    6       <H >        <3 >       <5 >       <3.0000>       <3.0000>       <3.0000>
    7       <F >        <4 >       <5 >       <4.0000>       <5.0000>       <6.0000>
    8       <G >        <4 >       <7 >       <3.0000>       <4.0000>       <8.0000>
    9       <I >        <5 >       <6 >       <7.0000>       <9.0000>       <12.000>
   10       <J >        <5 >       <7 >       <10.000>       <11.000>       <12.000>
   11       <K >        <6 >       <8 >       <6.0000>       <8.0000>       <11.000>
   12       <L >        <7 >       <8 >       <8.0000>       <10.000>       <12.000>
```

FIGURE 10.6. Screen display of each activity.

Step 5. You have the option of modifying the data as needed. This gives the menu displayed in Fig. 10.7.

```
                 Option Menu for Modifying CONSTR
        Option
            1    ----   Modify durations
            2    ----   Add one activity
            3    ----   Delete one activity
            4    ----   Display and/or print input data
            5    ----   Return to the function menu
```

FIGURE 10.7. Option menu for modifying a PERT problem.

Step 6. You are now ready to solve the problem. Select option 5 from the function menu. This will call up the solution menu, displayed in Fig. 10.8. Note that if you select option 1 from the solution menu, you will see intermediate results on the screen. These are shown in Figs. 10.9 and 10.10.

```
                 Option Menu for Solving CONSTR
   When solving a problem, you have the option of displaying the
intermediate results of the PERT method.  Also you can choose to
perform probability analysis if your project has some prespecified
schedules.  Your PERT program can display up to 10 critical paths if
your project network has multiple critical paths.

        Option
            1    ----   Solve and display the intermediate results
            2    ----   Solve without displaying any result
            3    ----   Print the final solution
            4    ----   Perform probability analysis
            5    ----   Return to the function menu
```

FIGURE 10.8. Option menu for solving a PERT problem.

Program Evaluation and Review Technique

```
                    PERT Analysis for CONSTR     Page  1
Activity    Activity        Earliest   Latest    Earliest  Latest    Slack
No. Name    Exp.Tm.  Var.   Start      Start     Finish    Finish    LS-ES
 1   A      5.0000   0.4444    0       1.8333    5.0000    6.8333    1.8333
 2   B      4.1667   0.0278    0       5.6667    4.1667    9.8333    5.6667
 3   C      7.8333   0.6944    0       0         7.8333    7.8333    Critical
 4   D      3.0000   0.1111    5.0000  6.8333    8.0000    9.8333    1.8333
 5   E      7.0000   0.4444    5.0000  18.667    12.000    25.667    13.667
 6   H      3.0000   0         8.0000  9.8333    11.000    12.833    1.8333
 7   F      5.0000   0.1111    7.8333  7.8333    12.833    12.833    Critical
 8   G      4.5000   0.6944    7.8333  19.333    12.333    23.833    11.500
 9   I      9.1667   0.6944    12.833  16.500    22.000    25.667    3.6667
10   J      11.000   0.1111    12.833  12.833    23.833    23.833    Critical
11   K      8.1667   0.6944    22.000  25.667    30.167    33.833    3.6667
12   L      10.000   0.4444    23.833  23.833    33.833    33.833    Critical
            Expected completion time = 33.83334
```

FIGURE 10.9. PERT analysis for the construction project.

```
Critical paths for CONSTR   with completion time =   33.83334

CP # 1  :  (with variance =   1.361111   )
        C              F             J              L
    1———————> 4———————> 5———————> 7———————> 8
```

FIGURE 10.10. Critical path.

You may select option 4 from the solution menu and perform probability analysis to find the probability that the project will be finished within 30, 33, or 35 days. This is illustrated in Fig. 10.11.

```
                Probability Analysis for CONSTR

   The following probability calculations assume that activities are
independent and that all paths are also independent.  It also assumes that
your network has a large enough number of activities so as to enable use of
the normal distribution.  Therefore, when the activities are not independent
or the number of activities is not large, the following analysis may be
highly biased.
Expected completion time =  33.83334
What is your project schedule time (type 0 to end analysis) ? 30

   On CP #  1 :    Variance =  1.361111    Standard deviation =   1.166667
      Probability of finishing within   30  is   5.112886E-04

The probability of finishing the whole project within  30  is  5.112886E-04

Do you want to enter a new scheduled completion time (Y/N)? Y

What is your project schedule time (type 0 to end analysis) ? 33

   On CP #  1 :    Variance =  1.361111    Standard deviation =   1.166667
      Probability of finishing within   33  is   .2375311
```

FIGURE 10.11. Probability analysis.

CHAPTER 10

```
The probability of finishing the whole project within  33  is  .2375311

Do you want to enter a new scheduled completion time (Y/N)?Y

What is your project schedule time (type 0 to end analysis) ? 35

   On CP # 1 :    Variance =  1.361111    Standard deviation =  1.166667
       Probability of finishing within  35  is  .8413508

The probability of finishing the whole project within  35  is  .8413508

Do you want to enter a new scheduled completion time (Y/N)?N

Analysis complete.
```

FIGURE 10.11 *(cont.)* Probability analysis.

Step 7. After the problem has been solved, you may use option 8 in the function menu to display or print the final solution. The menu of options available for displaying or printing is shown in Fig. 10.12. If you choose option 2 from this menu, then the final analysis and critical path are displayed and automatically printed, as shown in Figs. 10.9 and 10.10.

```
Option Menu for Displaying and/or Printing the Final Solution to CONSTR
      You have the following options available for displaying
      or printing the final solution.  If you want to print the
      solution, make sure that the printer is ready.

          Option

              1  ----  Display the final solution only
              2  ----  Display and print the final solution
              3  ----  Return to the function menu
```

FIGURE 10.12. Option menu for displaying and printing PERT solution.

Step 8. By choosing option 6 from the function menu, you can save the problem on a data disk(ette). Make sure that your data disk(ette) is formatted and inserted in the disk(ette) drive. Figure 10.13 gives the screen display for saving this problem.

```
                Decide on a file name for saving your problem.
            The file name may be the same as the problem name.
         Type x:xxxxxxxx.xxx for your file name ( e.g., A:XYZ.DAT ).

What is your file name (Type A:, B:, or C: to see all the files) ? a:CONSTR.dat
```

FIGURE 10.13. Screen display for saving a problem.

Exercises

1. Perform the PERT analysis for the following AOA network. The numbers on each arc are three time estimates for each activity.

Program Evaluation and Review Technique

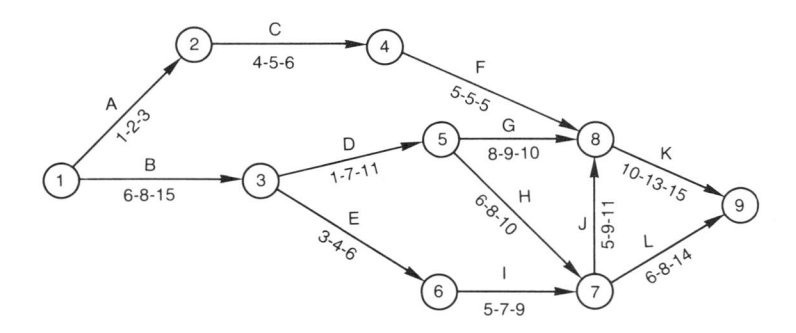

2. Consider the following AOA network. Assume that the optimistic time, most likely time, and pessimistic time of each activity are shown in the table. Find the probability of finishing the project within 55 days.

Activity	Optimistic time	Most likely time	Pessimistic time
A	5 days	6 days	8 days
B	1	7	11
C	3	3	3
D	4	4	6
E	1	2	3
F	6	8	9
G	4	5	6
H	3	4	5
I	6	6	7
J	7	8	9
K	11	12	13
L	5	5	5
M	3	3	5
N	10	12	13
O	9	11	14
P	4	6	8
Q	1	2	3
R	2	3	4
S	6	7	8
T	9	9	10
U	11	11	11
V	5	6	9
W	4	6	8
X	3	4	4
Y	1	2	3
Z	5	7	8

CHAPTER 10

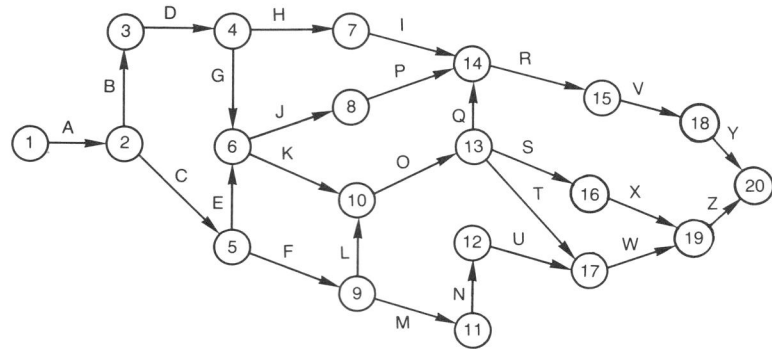

3. The following project to develop an orbiting solar collector has been funded by NASA as its contribution to the nation's energy crisis. The time estimates are in months.

Activity	Immediate predecessor	Optimistic time	Most likely time	Pessimistic time
A	—	4	6	8
B	—	1	2	3
C	A	4	4	4
D	A	4	5	6
E	B	7	10	16
F	B	8	9	10
G	C	2	2	2
H	D,E,G	2	3	7
I	F	1	3	11

a. Draw an AOA network.
b. What is the critical path?
c. Determine the probability of finishing the project within 18 months.

4. The following PERT network describes the sequence of activities necessary for carrying out a project. Activity durations are written on the arrows in the sequence of optimistic time, most likely time, and pessimistic time.

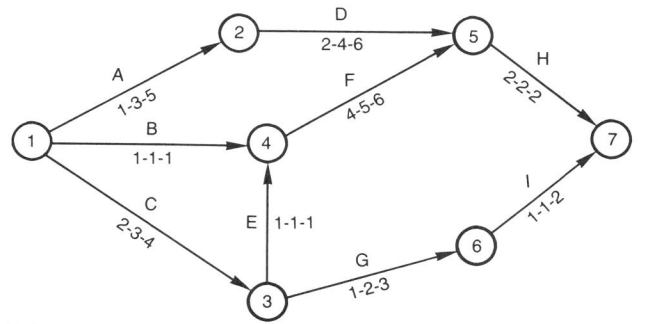

Determine ES, EF, LS, LF, and slack time for each activity. What is the critical path? Using the PERT approach, what is the probability of completing the project by 10 time units?

Program Evaluation and Review Technique

5. The following is an AOA network for carrying out a project. The durations of activities are stochastic and are recorded on the arcs by the sequence of optimistic, most likely, and pessimistic times. The durations are given in working days. The scheduled completion time of the project is ten working days.

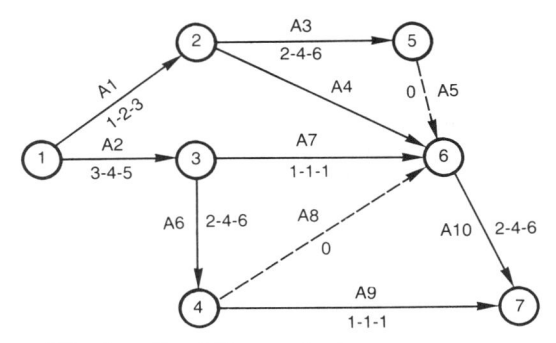

   a. Find the critical path of the project.
   b. Determine the probability of completing the project on or before the scheduled completion time.
   c. If the project is delayed beyond its scheduled completion time, a fixed penalty cost of $1000 would be incurred. We are given the opportunity to keep the scheduled completion time (10 days) or to extend the scheduled completion time to 12 days. The extension would require a renegotiated contract that would cost $200. Should the contract be renegotiated?

6. The following AOA network indicates the sequence of activities for completing a project. Activity durations are written below the arcs and are given in days.
   a. Perform the PERT analysis and find the critical path.
   b. Determine the probability of the project taking more than 16 days.
   c. Assume that the scheduled project time is 16 days. If the project is late, a penalty of $5000 will be incurred. However, we have been offered the opportunity to extend the scheduled time to 18 days, but this will cost us $300 for renegotiating the contract. Should the contract be renegotiated?
   d. Assume that we want to sign a contract that specifies the completion date of the project. We want to specify a completion date such that we are 95 percent certain of meeting or beating it. What completion date should be specified in the contract?

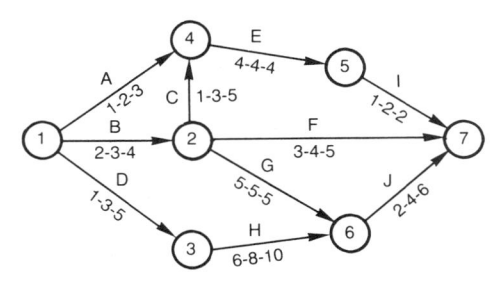

Chapter 11
DYNAMIC PROGRAMMING (DP)

Overview of the DP Decision Support System

This program contains three well-known dynamic programming algorithms: the stagecoach problem, the knapsack problem, and a production and inventory control problem. DP can solve these problems with up to 20 stages and up to 50 states for each stage. The solution procedure uses backward recursion from the last stage—that is, the stage closest to the destination—to the first stage.

The data required for the stagecoach problem are the number of stages, the number of states for each stage, and the distances between states on successive stages. For the knapsack problem, the space requirements and return values for each stage are required. The data required for the production/inventory control problem are demand, storage capacity with associated unit cost, production capacity with associated unit cost, and setup cost for each stage. The stage transformation function and return function used in this program are assumed to be linear. The problem can be saved on or read from a disk(ette).

After the data have been entered, you may choose options to solve the problems and display the results. Press the F8 key to print the output on the screen.

Special Notes on the DP Program

1. When entering a problem, use the BACKSPACE key to move the cursor to the position where you want to make a correction.

2. The DP program is designed to solve three types of popular dynamic programming problems with up to 20 stages and each stage with up to 50 states: the stagecoach problem, the knapsack problem, and a production and inventory control problem.

3. The data entry for the DP program is by the question and answer method.

4. The DP program can display a detailed decision and return table for each stage. The tables will contain enough information for you to inspect the dynamic programming solution process.

5. The solution in the DP program is backward, that is, the last stage is solved first.

Solving Problems with DP

When you first select DP, the function menu, shown in Fig. 11.1, will appear. You can now select the appropriate option. The steps for using DP to solve a dynamic programming problem are listed below:

```
        Welcome to your Dynamic Programming (DP) Decision Support System!
                 The options available for DP are as follows.
        If you are a first-time user, you might benefit from option 1.

        Option                    Function

           1        ----    Overview of DP Decision Support System
           2        ----    Enter new problem
           3        ----    Read existing problem from disk(ette)
           4        ----    Display and/or print input data
           5        ----    Solve problem
           6        ----    Save problem on disk(ette)
           7        ----    Modify problem
           8        ----    Display and/or print final solution
           9        ----    Return to the program menu
           0        ----    Exit from QSB
```

FIGURE 11.1. Function menu of the DP program.

1. Analyze the problem: define stages and states.

2. Enter the problem into QSB (use option 2) or read the existing problem from a data disk(ette) (use option 3).

3. Display or print the problem if you want to check and verify data (use option 4).

4. Modify the problem as necessary (use option 7).

5. Solve the problem by displaying or without displaying steps (use option 5).

6. Display and print the final solution (use option 8).

7. Save the problem on a data disk(ette) if you may need it again (use option 6).

8. If you want to solve other problems, go to step 3. Otherwise, return to the program menu (use option 9) to select another program or exit from QSB (use option 0).

Examples

To demonstrate the use of DP, consider the following example problems.

CHAPTER 11

Stagecoach Problem

Figure 11.2 displays a typical stagecoach problem. The number on each branch (arc) represents the distance between nodes. What is the shortest route from node 1 to node 10? Here are the steps to solve this problem using the DP program.

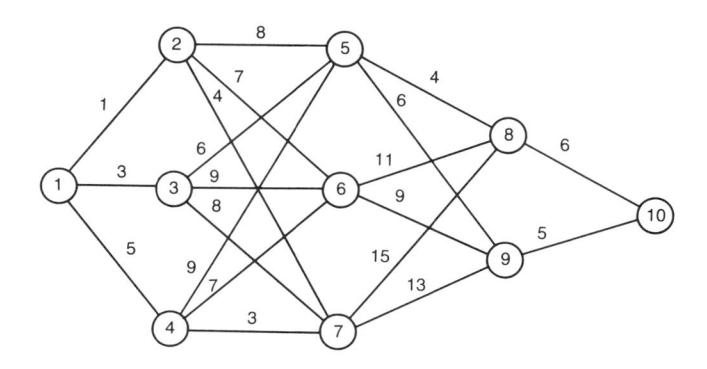

FIGURE 11.2. Network of the stagecoach problem.

Step 1. Analyze the problem: define stages and states. As in conventional stagecoach problems, we define four stages for the problem shown in Fig. 11.2. Stage 1 represents the arcs closest to the source node (node 1), stage 2 represents the arcs next closest to the source node, and so on. The input nodes of arcs are defined as states for each stage.

Step 2. Enter the problem (the data underlined in the following figures will be entered into DP):

2.1. Enter problem name and number of stages shown in Fig. 11.3.

```
Please name your problem using up to 6 characters ? STGCH
Your DP program can analyze problems with up to 20 stages and with up to
900 states in total.  Specifically, the program can solve problems with up
to 2800 branches (arcs) for stagecoach problems.
How many stages ( ≤ 20 ) are there in your problem ? 4
```

FIGURE 11.3. Screen display for defining problem name and number of stages.

2.2. Select one of the three options shown in Fig. 11.4 to specify your problem. Note the conventions that appear on the screen (Fig. 11.5) when you enter data.

Dynamic Programming

```
Select one of the following algorithms:

    1 -- Stagecoach Problem
    2 -- Knapsack Problem
    3 -- Production and Inventory Control Problem
    4 -- Return to the function menu

Enter the option number ? 1
```

FIGURE 11.4. Screen display of DP for selecting problems.

```
Please observe the following conventions when entering a problem:

    (1) The stage closest to the source is defined as stage 1, and the
        stage closest to the destination is defined as the last stage.
    (2) The following questions are designed to match your special DP problem.
    (3) The Esc key allows you to reenter data from the beginning.
    (4) The / key allows you to reenter the data of the previous question.
    (5) After entering a problem, the function menu allows you to modify data.
```

FIGURE 11.5. Screen display of conventions for DP problem entry.

2.3. Figure 11.6 displays the screen for entering distances of arcs.

```
                  Entry for Stagecoach Problem STGCH

    The following entry will begin with the first stage, which is
    from the source node.  The nodes will be automatically numbered
    beginning with 1 from the first stage (source) to the last stage.

Stage  1 :

    How many output nodes for this stage? 3
    The output nodes will be numbered from 2 to 4

          From input node 1    to output node 2 :  Distance/Cost? 1
          From input node 1    to output node 3 :  Distance/Cost? 3
          From input node 1    to output node 4 :  Distance/Cost? 5

Stage  2 :

    How many output nodes for this stage? 3
    The output nodes will be numbered from 5 to 7

          From input node 2    to output node 5 :  Distance/Cost? 8
          From input node 2    to output node 6 :  Distance/Cost? 7
          From input node 2    to output node 7 :  Distance/Cost? 4
          From input node 3    to output node 5 :  Distance/Cost? 6
          From input node 3    to output node 6 :  Distance/Cost? 9
          From input node 3    to output node 7 :  Distance/Cost? 8
          From input node 4    to output node 5 :  Distance/Cost? 9
          From input node 4    to output node 6 :  Distance/Cost? 7
          From input node 4    to output node 7 :  Distance/Cost? 3
```

FIGURE 11.6. Screen display for entering the stagecoach problem.

CHAPTER 11

```
Stage  3  :

    How many output nodes for this stage? 2
    The output nodes will be numbered from 8 to  9

        From input node 5  to output node 8 :  Distance/Cost? 4
        From input node 5  to output node 9 :  Distance/Cost? 6
        From input node 6  to output node 8 :  Distance/Cost? 11
        From input node 6  to output node 9 :  Distance/Cost? 9
        From input node 7  to output node 8 :  Distance/Cost? 15
        From input node 7  to output node 9 :  Distance/Cost? 13

Stage  4  :

    How many output nodes for this stage? 1
    The output nodes will be numbered from 10 to  10

        From input node 8  to output node 10 :  Distance/Cost? 6
        From input node 9  to output node 10 :  Distance/Cost? 5
```

FIGURE 11.6 *(cont.)* Screen display for entering the stagecoach problem.

Step 3. You may display or print the entered data, as shown in Fig. 11.7.

```
Stage  1  :

        From input node 1  to output node 2 :  Distance/Cost=  1
        From input node 1  to output node 3 :  Distance/Cost=  3
        From input node 1  to output node 4 :  Distance/Cost=  5

Stage  2  :

        From input node 2  to output node 5 :  Distance/Cost=  8
        From input node 2  to output node 6 :  Distance/Cost=  7
        From input node 2  to output node 7 :  Distance/Cost=  4
        From input node 3  to output node 5 :  Distance/Cost=  6
        From input node 3  to output node 6 :  Distance/Cost=  9
        From input node 3  to output node 7 :  Distance/Cost=  8
        From input node 4  to output node 5 :  Distance/Cost=  9
        From input node 4  to output node 6 :  Distance/Cost=  7
        From input node 4  to output node 7 :  Distance/Cost=  3

Stage  3  :

        From input node 5  to output node 8 :  Distance/Cost=  4
        From input node 5  to output node 9 :  Distance/Cost=  6
        From input node 6  to output node 8 :  Distance/Cost=  11
        From input node 6  to output node 9 :  Distance/Cost=  9
        From input node 7  to output node 8 :  Distance/Cost=  15
        From input node 7  to output node 9 :  Distance/Cost=  13

Stage  4  :

        From input node 8  to output node 10 :  Distance/Cost=  6
        From input node 9  to output node 10 :  Distance/Cost=  5
```

FIGURE 11.7. Screen display of the stagecoach problem.

Step 4. You have the option of modifying the problem as needed. This gives the menu displayed in Fig. 11.8.

Dynamic Programming

```
              Option Menu for Modifying STGCH
     Option

        1   ----    Modify the stagecoach problem
        2   ----    Modify the knapsack problem
        3   ----    Modify the production/inventory problem
        4   ----    Display and/or print input data
        5   ----    Return to the function menu
```

FIGURE 11.8. Option menu for modifying a problem.

Step 5. You are now ready to solve the problem. Select option 5 from the function menu. This will call up the solution menu displayed in Fig. 11.9. Note that if you select option 1 from the solution menu, you will see every iteration on the screen. These iterations are shown in Fig. 11.10.

```
              Option Menu for Solving STGCH
    When solving a problem, you have the option of displaying the DP
   table of each stage.  Also you may choose to print the final solution.

     Option

        1   ----    Solve and display each step
        2   ----    Solve without displaying steps
        3   ----    Print the final solution
        4   ----    Return to the function menu
```

FIGURE 11.9. Option menu for solving a problem.

```
Detailed Steps for the Stagecoach Problem:
Stage  4 :

    Input Node       Arc Decision       Output Node      Distance to Destination
         8              8 - 10              10                   6
         9              9 - 10              10                   5
Stage  3 :

    Input Node       Arc Decision       Output Node      Distance to Destination
         5              5 - 8               8                   10
         6              6 - 9               9                   14
         7              7 - 9               9                   18
Stage  2 :

    Input Node       Arc Decision       Output Node      Distance to Destination
         2              2 - 5               5                   18
         3              3 - 5               5                   16
         4              4 - 5               5                   19
```

FIGURE 11.10. Detailed iterations for the stagecoach problem.

CHAPTER 11

```
Stage  1 :
    Input Node      Arc Decision       Output Node     Distance to Destination
        1              1 - 2                2                    19
```

FIGURE 11.10 *(cont.)* Detailed iterations for the stagecoach problem.

Step 6. After the problem has been solved, you may use option 8 in the function menu to display or print the final solution. The menu of options available for displaying or printing is shown in Fig. 11.11. If you choose option 2 from this menu, the final solution is displayed and automatically printed, as shown in Fig. 11.12.

```
Option Menu for Displaying and/or Printing the Final Solution to STGCH
       You have the following options available for displaying
     or printing the final solution.  If you want to print the
     solution, make sure that the printer is ready.

       Option
          1    ----   Display the final solution only
          2    ----   Display and print the final solution
          3    ----   Return to the function menu
```

FIGURE 11.11. Option menu for displaying/printing stagecoach problem solution.

```
            The Final Shortest Routes for STGCH
       Stage      Arc Decision    Distance to Destination
         4           1 - 2                  19
         3           2 - 5                  18
         2           5 - 8                  10
         1           8 - 10                  6
```

FIGURE 11.12. The final solution of the stagecoach problem.

Step 7. By choosing option 6 from the function menu, you can save the problem on a data disk(ette). Make sure that your data disk(ette) is formatted and inserted in the disk(ette) drive. Figure 11.13 gives the screen display for saving your problem.

```
              Decide on a file name for saving your problem.
               The file name may be the same as the problem name.
             Type x:xxxxxxxx.xxx for your file name ( e.g., A:XYZ.DAT ).
What is your file name (Type A:, B:, or C: to see all the files) ? a:STGCH.dat
```

FIGURE 11.13. Screen display for saving a problem.

Dynamic Programming

Knapsack Problem

The following example demonstrates the procedure to solve a knapsack problem using the DP program. A salesman travels around the country with his van to sell different kinds of goods. The van has 20 units in space. For a specific trip, the salesman has four different types of goods to carry. Each type of goods has limited available units, requires different units of space, and provides a different profit for the salesman. Table 11.1 displays this information. Suppose that the salesman can sell what he carries. Suggest how the salesman can maximize his profit for this trip.

Table 11.1. Related information for the salesman's next trip

Types of goods	Unit available	Space required per unit	Profit per unit
A	5	10	8
B	3	6	10
C	4	3	4
D	2	5	7

The procedure to enter the data for this problem is shown in Figs. 11.14 and 11.15, and the solution process displaying each iteration is shown in Figs. 11.16 to 11.21.

```
Please name your problem using up to 6 characters ? SLSMAN
Your DP program can analyze problems with up to 20 stages and with up to
900 states in total.  Specifically, the program can solve problems with up
to 2800 branches (arcs) for stagecoach problems.
How many stages ( ≤ 20 ) are there in your problem ? 4
    Select one of the following algorithms:

    1 -- Stagecoach Problem
    2 -- Knapsack Problem
    3 -- Production and Inventory Control Problem
    4 -- Return to the function menu
    Enter the option number ? 2
```

FIGURE 11.14. Screen display for selecting knapsack problem.

```
                Entry for Knapsack Problem SLSMAN

    The following entry will begin with the first stage, which is the
    first type of item.  Each stage represents one type of item.  The
    data required are capacity of knapsack, maximum number for each
    type of item, space required for each type of item, weight(value)
    for each type of item.
```

FIGURE 11.15. Screen display for entering the knapsack problem.

CHAPTER 11

```
What is the capacity of knapsack ? 20

Stage (Type of Item) 1 :
    What is the maximum number ( ≤50 )of type of item  1     ? 5
    What is the space required for each of this type of item ? 10
    What is the weight (value) for each of this type of item ? 8

Stage (Type of Item) 2 :
    What is the maximum number ( ≤50 )of type of item  2     ? 3
    What is the space required for each of this type of item ? 6
    What is the weight (value) for each of this type of item ? 10

Stage (Type of Item) 3 :
    What is the maximum number ( ≤50 )of type of item  3     ? 4
    What is the space required for each of this type of item ? 3
    What is the weight (value) for each of this type of item ? 4

Stage (Type of Item) 4 :
    What is the maximum number ( ≤50 )of type of item  4     ? 2
    What is the space required for each of this type of item ? 5
    What is the weight (value) for each of this type of item ? 7
```

FIGURE 11.15 *(cont.)* Screen display for entering the knapsack problem.

```
                    Capacity of Knapsack =  20
Type of Item (Stage)    Number of Items     Space Required     Weight/Value
        1                     5                  10                 8
        2                     3                   6                10
        3                     4                   3                 4
        4                     2                   5                 7
```

FIGURE 11.16. Screen display for the knapsack problem.

```
Stage (Type of Item) 4 :

    Input State    Decision    Output State    Maximum Return Value
        0             0             0                   0
        1             0             1                   0
        2             0             2                   0
        3             0             3                   0
        4             0             4                   0
        5             1             0                   7
        6             1             1                   7
        7             1             2                   7
        8             1             3                   7
        9             1             4                   7
       10             2             0                  14
       11             2             1                  14
       12             2             2                  14
       13             2             3                  14
       14             2             4                  14
       15             2             5                  14
       16             2             6                  14
       17             2             7                  14
       18             2             8                  14
       19             2             9                  14
       20             2            10                  14
```

FIGURE 11.17. Screen display for stage 4 of the salesman problem.

Dynamic Programming

```
Stage (Type of Item) 3 :

    Input State      Decision      Output State     Maximum Return Value
        0               0               0                  0
        1               0               1                  0
        2               0               2                  0
        3               1               0                  4
        4               1               1                  4
        5               0               5                  7
        6               2               0                  8
        7               2               1                  8
        8               1               5                 11
        9               3               0                 12
       10               0              10                 14
       11               2               5                 15
       12               4               0                 16
       13               1              10                 18
       14               3               5                 19
       15               3               6                 19
       16               2              10                 22
       17               4               5                 23
       18               4               6                 23
       19               3              10                 26
       20               3              11                 26
```

FIGURE 11.18. Screen display for stage 3 of the salesman problem.

```
Stage (Type of Item) 2 :

    Input State      Decision      Output State     Maximum Return Value
        0               0               0                  0
        1               0               1                  0
        2               0               2                  0
        3               0               3                  4
        4               0               4                  4
        5               0               5                  7
        6               1               0                 10
        7               1               1                 10
        8               0               8                 11
        9               1               3                 14
       10               0              10                 14
       11               1               5                 17
       12               2               0                 20
       13               2               1                 20
       14               1               8                 21
       15               2               3                 24
       16               1              10                 24
       17               2               5                 27
       18               3               0                 30
       19               3               1                 30
       20               2               8                 31
```

FIGURE 11.19. Screen display for stage 2 of the salesman problem.

```
Stage (Type of Item) 1 :

    Input State      Decision      Output State     Maximum Return Value
       20               0              20                 31
```

FIGURE 11.20. Screen display for stage 1 of the salesman problem.

CHAPTER 11

```
              The Final Solution for SLSMAN
     Stage   Decision   Return   Capacity Left
       1        0         0           20
       2        2        20            8
       3        1         4            5
       4        1         7            0

              Total Return = 31
```

FIGURE 11.21. Screen display for final solution of the salesman problem.

Production and Inventory Control Problem

The following example demonstrates the procedure to solve a production and inventory control problem using the DP program. BBC produces tailored-made space shuttle components. For the next four months, BBC has to deliver one kind of special component. Table 11.2 shows the related production and inventory information for the next four months. If BBC does not have inventory right now, what is the best production schedule for BBC to implement to minimize total cost while meeting the demand?

Table 11.2. Production and inventory information for BBC

Month	Demand	Production capacity	Storage capacity	Production setup cost	Unit production cost	Unit holding cost
Jan.	4	6	4	$500	$300	$100
Feb.	5	4	3	450	320	100
Mar.	3	7	2	500	250	120
Apr.	4	5	4	600	350	140

Data entry with DP for this problem is shown in Figs. 11.22 and 11.23, and the solution process displaying each iteration is shown in Figs. 11.24 to 11.29.

```
Please name your problem using up to 6 characters ? BBC

Your DP program can analyze problems with up to 20 stages and with up to

900 states in total.  Specifically, the program can solve problems with up

to 2800 branches (arcs) for stagecoach problems.

How many stages ( ≤ 20 ) are there in your problem ? 4
    Select one of the following algorithms:

        1 -- Stagecoach Problem
        2 -- Knapsack Problem
        3 -- Production and Inventory Control Problem
        4 -- Return to the function menu

    Enter the option number ? 3
```

FIGURE 11.22. Screen display for selecting production/inventory problem.

Dynamic Programming

```
            Entry for Production and Inventory Control Problem BBC

      The following entry will begin with the first stage, which is the
      first control period. Each stage represents one period. The
      data required are demand, production/purchasing capacity, storage
      capacity, setup cost, production/purchasing cost per unit,
      holding cost per unit for each period, and the initial inventory.

How many units of initial inventory ? 0

Stage (Period) 1 :

    What is the demand ( ≤50 ) for this period ? 4
    What is the production capacity for this period ? 6
    What is the storage capacity for this period ? 4
    What is the setup cost for this period ? 500
    What is the unit production cost for this period ? 300
    What is the unit holding cost for this period ? 100

Stage (Period) 2 :

    What is the demand ( ≤50 ) for this period ? 5
    What is the production capacity for this period ? 4
    What is the storage capacity for this period ? 3
    What is the setup cost for this period ? 450
    What is the unit production cost for this period ? 320
    What is the unit holding cost for this period ? 100

Stage (Period) 3 :

    What is the demand ( ≤50 ) for this period ? 3
    What is the production capacity for this period ? 7
    What is the storage capacity for this period ? 2
    What is the setup cost for this period ? 500
    What is the unit production cost for this period ? 250
    What is the unit holding cost for this period ? 120

Stage (Period) 4 :

    What is the demand ( ≤50 ) for this period ? 4
    What is the production capacity for this period ? 5
    What is the storage capacity for this period ? 4
    What is the setup cost for this period ? 600
    What is the unit production cost for this period ? 350
    What is the unit holding cost for this period ? 140
```

FIGURE 11.23. Screen display for entering production/inventory problem.

```
      Input Data Describing Your Problem BBC -- Production/Inventory Problem

                        Initial Inventory =   0
```

Period (Stage)	Demand	Production Capacity	Storage Capacity	Setup Cost	Production Unit Cost	Holding Unit Cost
1	4	6	4	500	300	100
2	5	4	3	450	320	100
3	3	7	2	500	250	120
4	4	5	4	600	350	140

FIGURE 11.24. Screen display for production/inventory problem.

CHAPTER 11

```
Stage (Period) 4 :
    Input Inventory      Production      Output Inventory      Minimum Total Cost
            0                4                    0                   2000
            1                3                    0                   1650
            2                2                    0                   1300
```

FIGURE 11.25. Screen display for stage 4 of production/inventory problem.

```
Stage (Period) 3 :
    Input Inventory      Production      Output Inventory      Minimum Total Cost
            0                3                    0                   3250
            1                2                    0                   3000
            2                1                    0                   2750
            3                0                    0                   2000
```

FIGURE 11.26. Screen display for stage 3 of production/inventory problem.

```
Stage (Period) 2 :
    Input Inventory      Production      Output Inventory      Minimum Total Cost
            0                0                   -5                 Infeasible
            1                4                    0                   4980
            2                3                    0                   4660
            3                2                    0                   4340
            4                1                    0                   4020
```

FIGURE 11.27. Screen display for stage 2 of production/inventory problem.

```
Stage (Period) 1 :
    Input Inventory      Production      Output Inventory      Minimum Total Cost
            0                5                    1                   7080
```

FIGURE 11.28. Screen display for stage 1 of production/inventory problem.

```
                        The Final Solution for BBC

Period   Beginning   Production   Setup   Production   Ending      Holding   Total
(Stage)  Inventory                Cost    Cost         Inventory   Cost      Cost

  1          0           5        500     1500            1         100      2100
  2          1           4        450     1280            0           0      1730
  3          0           3        500      750            0           0      1250
  4          0           4        600     1400            0           0      2000

                           Total Cost = 7080
```

FIGURE 11.29. The final solution of BBC production/inventory problem.

Dynamic Programming

Exercises

1. Consider the network shown below. The numbers on the arcs are distances in miles. What is the shortest route from node 1 to node 16?

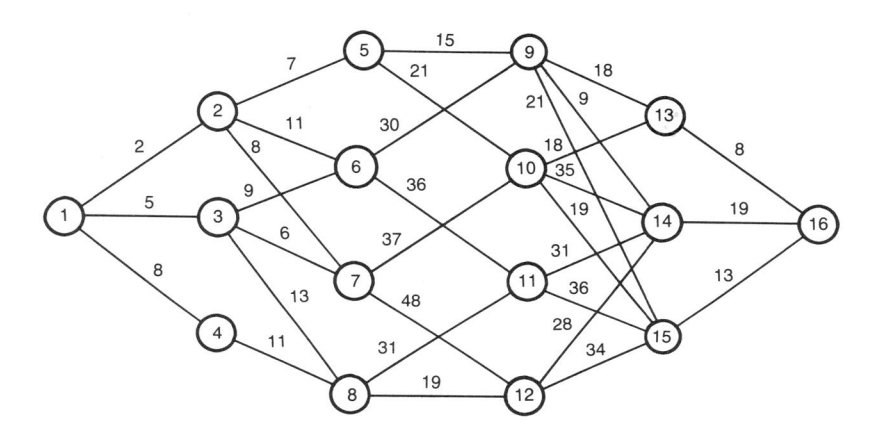

2. Consider the network shown below. Assume that the number on each arc is the travel time in minutes. What is the shortest time to travel from city 1 to city 25?

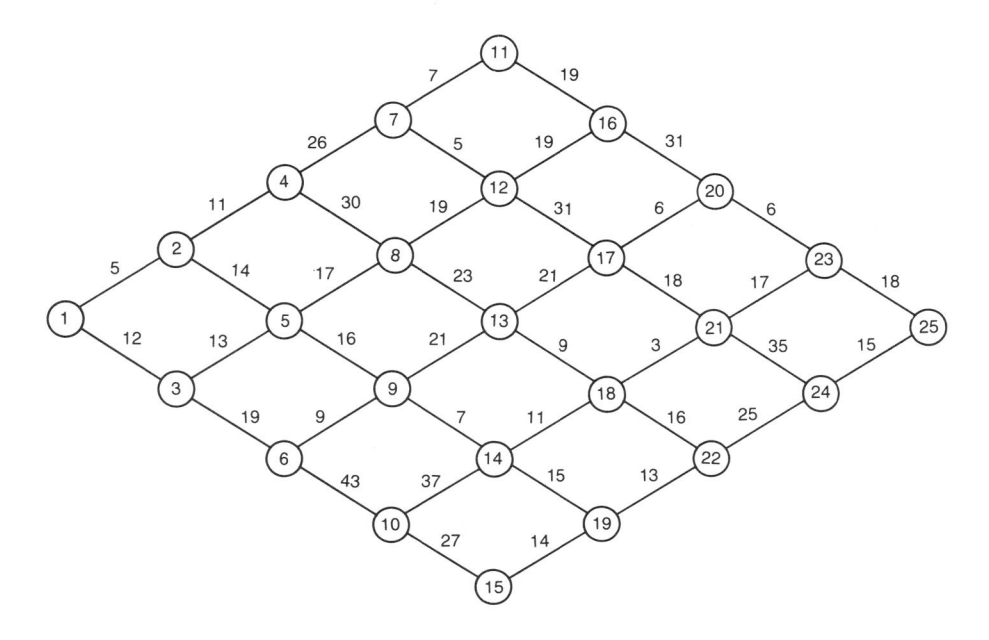

3. A local retail shop has available a 6 ft x 3 ft x 2 ft display area for cosmetics products. The shop must determine which of its top ten target products to place on the

display area. The unit profits and unit space requirements are given below. The space requirements are expressed in cubic feet, which include the surrounding space for an attractive visual effect.

Product:	1	2	3	4	5	6	7	8	9	10
Profit:	$3	2	1	5	9	7	4	6	4	8
Space:	5	6	3	7	13	15	7	9	6	18

Recommend a solution for this display decision.

4. You have $30,000 to take advantage of an investment opportunity. The following table lists the stock alternatives and related information. How would you allocate your $30,000? Assume the purchase of stocks is in units of a thousand.

Alternative	Cost per unit	Available in thousand	Expected profit per unit
Stock 1	$2	5	$1
Stock 2	4	6	1.8
Stock 3	3	2	1.9
Stock 4	5	7	2
Stock 5	8	4	2.1

5. The following table lists information related to a production and inventory control situation. If the initial inventory is two units, determine a production plan to minimize the total cost.

Month	Demand	Production capacity	Storage capacity	Production setup cost	Unit production cost	Unit holding cost
1	10	12	5	$1000	$200	$ 80
2	12	14	5	1100	210	100
3	15	13	5	1100	220	90
4	6	14	10	1200	210	80
5	7	13	8	1500	250	100
6	8	10	5	1400	240	110

6. Jeming Industries, Inc., produces high-power transformers to industries. For the next ten months, the company has the following demands: 1, 2, 7, 6, 5, 3, 4, 5, 6, 2. According to the unstable labor market, the company can produce at most 4, 5, 6, 7, 8, 7, 4, 6, 4, and 3 units, respectively. The company has a stockroom that can hold 5 units of finished products. The current stock is 2 units. The production setup cost is $500 per setup and the variable production cost is $200 per unit. The carrying cost is $40 per unit per month. Assume that Jeming plans the production schedule month by month. Decide on a plan for the company to meet demand while minimizing the total cost.

Chapter 12
INVENTORY THEORY (INVT)

Overview of the INVT Decision Support System

This program enables you to evaluate three classic inventory problems: economic order quantity (EOQ), EOQ with discount analysis, and single-period stochastic systems (newsboy problems). The data required for EOQ are inventory holding costs, ordering costs, shortage costs, and value (cost) of an inventory unit. Additional data requirements are demand, replenishment rate, and lead time. For discount analysis, discounts and price breaks are required in addition to the EOQ data. The single-period stochastic problem requires selling price, salvage value, unit and shortage costs, and demand distribution. Demand distribution is assumed to be normal or discrete with fewer than 50 outcomes. You can enter a new problem, or you can read an existing problem from a disk(ette).

The INVT decision support system enables you to display, save, modify, and solve your inventory problems. You may display the cost function curves when solving an EOQ problem. After a problem is solved, the results will be displayed on the screen. By pressing the F8 key, you can print the output.

Special Notes on the INVT Program

1. When entering a problem, use the Esc key to reenter the data from the beginning, or the / key to reenter the previous question.

2. The INVT program will solve classic inventory problems, including economic order quantity (EOQ), deterministic discount analysis, and newsboy problems.

3. You can assign an order quantity and let the INVT program calculate the related inventory costs.

Solving Problems with INVT

When you first select INVT, the function menu, shown in Fig. 12.1, will appear. You can now select the appropriate option. The steps for using INVT to solve an inventory problem are listed below:

CHAPTER 12

```
       Welcome to your Inventory Model (INVT) Decision Support System!
              The options available for INVT are as follows.
     If you are a first-time user, you might benefit from option 1.

        Option                    Function

            1       ----    Overview of INVT Decision Support System
            2       ----    Enter new problem
            3       ----    Read existing problem from disk(ette)
            4       ----    Display and/or print input data
            5       ----    Solve problem
            6       ----    Save problem on disk(ette)
            7       ----    Modify problem
            9       ----    Return to the program menu
            0       ----    Exit from QSB
```

FIGURE 12.1. Function menu of the INVT program.

1. Analyze the problem and prepare the data.

2. Enter the problem into QSB (use option 2) or read the existing problem from a data disk(ette) (use option 3).

3. Display or print the problem if you want to check and verify data (use option 4).

4. Modify the problem as necessary (use option 7).

5. Solve the problem with display of results (use option 5).

6. Save the problem on a data disk(ette) if you may need it again (use option 6).

7. If you want to solve other problems, go to step 3. Otherwise, return to the program menu (use option 9) to select another program or exit from QSB (use option 0).

Examples

To demonstrate the use of INVT, consider the following example problems.

Economic Order Quantity

TV Shack is a local television retailer. From experience, the company knows that the demand for televisions is very steady with a mean of 50 sets per month and that the ordering cost is $50 per order. The annual holding cost, including capital cost and warehousing cost, is 20 percent of the purchasing price. The wholesaler offers a price of $300 per set. What is the best quantity that the retailer should order each time so that the inventory cost is minimized?

Step 1. Analyze the problem and prepare data for entry. The problem is a classic EOQ problem with:

Inventory Theory

Demand = (50)(12) = 600 per year
Ordering cost = $50 per order
Holding cost = (0.2)(300) = $60 per set per year
Unit cost = $300

Step 2. Enter the problem (the data underlined in the following figures will be entered into QSB):

2.1. Enter problem name and time unit, as shown in Fig. 12.2.

```
Please name your problem using up to 6 characters ? TVSHK

Please specify the time unit (e.g., day, week,...) (default = year) ? year
```

FIGURE 12.2. Screen display for entering problem name and time unit.

2.2. Select one of the three options shown in Fig. 12.3 to specify your problem. Note the conventions that appear on the screen when you enter data.

```
                    INVT Data Entry for TVSHK

Please observe the following conventions when entering a problem:
    (1) The Esc key allows you to reenter data from the beginning.
    (2) The / key allows you to reenter data for the previous question.
    (3) To enter the default value, just press the ENTER key.

        Select one of the options for entering your model:

            1 -- Deterministic Economic Order Quantity (EOQ)
            2 -- Deterministic discount analysis
            3 -- Single-period probabilistic demand problem
            0 -- Return to the function menu

        Please enter the option number ? 1
```

FIGURE 12.3. Screen display of INVT for selecting problems.

2.3. Fig. 12.4 displays the screen for entering inventory data.

```
                    EOQ Problem Entry for TVSHK

        Demand per year ? 600
        Order or setup cost per order ? 50
        Holding cost per unit per year ? 60
        Shortage cost per unit per year (default = ∞) ?
        Shortage cost per unit, independent of time (default = 0) ?
        Replenishment or production rate per year (default = ∞) ?
        Lead time for a new order in year (default = 0)?
        Unit cost ? 300
```

FIGURE 12.4. Screen display of INVT for entering an EOQ data.

115

Step 3. You may display or print the entered data, as shown in Fig. 12.5.

```
EOQ Input Data:
    Demand per year (D) = 600
    Order or setup cost per order (Co) = 50
    Holding cost per unit per year (Ch) = 60
    Shortage cost per unit per year (Cs) = ∞
    Shortage cost per unit, independent of time (π) = 0
    Replenishment or production rate per year (P) = ∞
    Lead time for a new order in year (LT) = 0
    Unit cost (C) = 300
```

FIGURE 12.5. Screen display of EOQ data.

Step 4. You have the option to modify the problem. This gives the menu displayed in Fig. 12.6.

```
                     Modify Inventory Data

You may change one of the following inventory data:

    1 -- Demand
    2 -- Order or set-up cost
    3 -- Holding cost
    4 -- Shortage cost per unit time
    5 -- Shortage cost independent of time
    6 -- Replenishment or production rate
    7 -- Lead time
    8 -- Unit cost
    9 -- Selling price
   10 -- Salvage value
   11 -- Shortage cost (newsboy problem)
   12 -- Display and/or print input data
    0 -- Return to the function menu

Enter the option number ?
```

FIGURE 12.6. Option menu for modifying inventory data.

Step 5. You are now ready to solve the problem. Select option 5 from the function menu. This will call up the solution menu displayed in Fig. 12.7. Note that if you select option 1 from the solution menu, you will see the EOQ and related information shown in Fig. 12.8; if you select option 2, you will have inventory costs plotted, as shown in Fig. 12.9. When you select option 1, you will have a choice to assign your order quantity.

Inventory Theory

```
                Option Menu for Solving TVSHK
  You have the following options available for solving the inventory
problem.  Options 1 and 2 are for EOQ, option 3 is for discount
analysis, option 4 is for probabilistic demand analysis.
```
```
           Option
              1    ----  EOQ/Inventory cost calculation
              2    ----  Display inventory cost curves
              3    ----  Discount analysis
              4    ----  Probabilistic demand analysis
              5    ----  Return to the function menu
```

FIGURE 12.7. Option menu for solving an inventory problem.

```
                     EOQ Results for TVSHK
    EOQ Input Data:
        Demand per year (D) =  600
        Order or setup cost per order (Co) =  50
        Holding cost per unit per year (Ch) =  60
        Shortage cost per unit per year (Cs) = ∞
        Shortage cost per unit, independent of time (π) = 0
        Replenishment or production rate per year (P) = ∞
        Lead time for a new order in year (LT) = 0
        Unit cost (C) = 300

    EOQ Output:
        EOQ                  =        31.623
        Maximum inventory    =        31.623
        Maximum backorder    =         0.000
        Order interval       =         0.053  year
        Reorder point        =         0.000
            Ordering cost    =       948.683
            Holding  cost    =       948.683
            Shortage cost    =         0.000
        Subtotal of inventory cost per year   =        1897.366
        Material cost per year                =      180000.000
        Total cost per year                   =      181897.359
```

FIGURE 12.8. Screen display for the TV Shack solution.

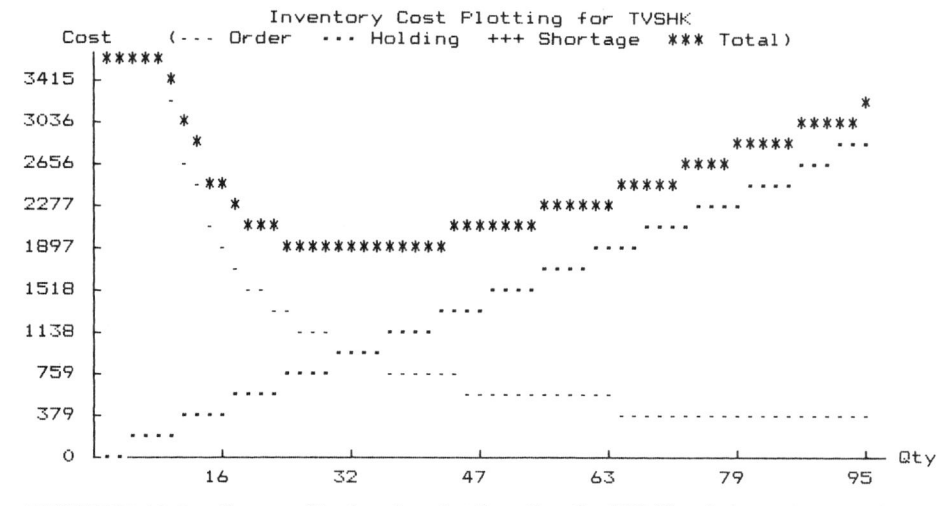

```
                Inventory Cost Plotting for TVSHK
      Cost    (--- Order   ··· Holding  +++ Shortage  *** Total)
              |*****
       3415   | *                                                            *
              |  *                                           *****
       3036   |   *                                       *****    ···
              |                                         ****    ···
       2656   |   -**                                 *****  ····
              |      *                           ******   ····
       2277   |    ***          **************      ····
       1897   |       -                              ····
              |         --                    ····
       1518   |           --               ····
              |             -           ···
       1138   |              ···     ····
              |                ··· ····
        759   |                 ····       ·········
              |           ····         ·············
        379   |      ····      ·················
              | ····
          0   |_____Qty
                      16       32      47      63      79      95
```

FIGURE 12.9. Screen display for plotting the the TV Shack inventory cost.

CHAPTER 12

Step 6. By choosing option 6 from the function menu, you can save the problem on a data disk(ette). Make sure that your data disk(ette) is formatted and inserted in the disk(ette) drive. Figure 12.10 gives the screen display for saving the problem.

```
              Decide on a file name for saving your problem.
              The file name may be the same as the problem name.
              Type x:xxxxxxxx.xxx for your file name ( e.g., A:XYZ.DAT ).

What is your file name (Type A:, B:, or C: to see all the files) ? a:TVSHK.dat
```

FIGURE 12.10. Screen display for saving the problem.

Price Discounts

If the wholesaler offers 2 percent and 5 percent discounts as TV Shack orders more than or equal to 50 sets and 80 sets, respectively, what is the best order strategy for TV Shack? The procedure to enter the data for this problem is shown in Figs. 12.11 and 12.12, and the solution process starting with option 3 in the solution menu is shown in Fig. 12.13.

```
                        INVT Data Entry for TVSHK

Please observe the following conventions when entering a problem:
     (1) The Esc key allows you to reenter data from the beginning.
     (2) The / key allows you to reenter data for the previous question.
     (3) To enter the default value, just press the ENTER key.

     Select one of the options for entering your model:

           1 -- Deterministic Economic Order Quantity (EOQ)
           2 -- Deterministic discount analysis
           3 -- Single-period probabilistic demand problem
           0 -- Return to the function menu

     Please enter the option number ? 2
```

FIGURE 12.11. Screen display for selecting discount analysis.

```
                   Discount Analysis Data Entry for TVSHK

     EOQ data is already in the system.
     Do you want to enter EOQ data again (Y/N) ? n

     How many discount breaks do you want to analyze ? 2

     Enter the discount breaks beginning with the first(lowest) price level:

     Discount break # 1
           Break quantity ? 50
           Discount (%) ? 2
     Discount break # 2
           Break quantity ? 80
           Discount (%) ? 5
```

FIGURE 12.12. Screen display for entering discount data.

```
                    Discount Analysis for TVSHK
Without discount:  EOQ =         31.623    Total cost =     181897.359

  Discount:  2.0%   Quantity :    50 --      80

      EOQ =    32   Total cost =  178278.297 ----> Infeasible
      Break =   50   Total cost =  178470.000 ----> Take and order this break.

  Discount:  5.0%   Quantity :    80 --       ∞

      EOQ =    32   Total cost =  172849.328 ----> Infeasible
      Break =   80   Total cost =  173655.000 ----> Take and order this break.

      Optimal decision: Discount  5 %   Order   80   Total cost = 173655
```

FIGURE 12.13. Screen display of discount analysis for TV Shack.

Exercises

1. Assume that a production system has the following related information:
   Annual demand = 1800 units
   Setup cost = $120
   Holding cost per year per unit = 20 percent of the unit production cost
   Unit production cost = $40
   Shortage cost per year per unit = $10
   Lead time = 0.01 year
   a. What is the EOQ?
   b. What are the related inventory costs?

2. Assume that the production rate is 300 units per month for problem 1. What are the effects on the questions of problem 1?

3. Given an inventory system with the following information:
   Annual demand = 120 units
   Ordering cost = $45
   Annual carrying cost per unit = $48
   Unit cost = $200
   a. What is the EOQ?
   b. What is the total inventory cost?
   c. The supplier offers a 2 percent discount on the unit price if the items are purchased in lots of 100 or more at one time. Should management accept the offer?

4. To produce the tape recorder doll, Educational Toy Company purchases all the doll material from the same vendor. The annual demand is 10,000 units, ordering cost is $10, and the holding cost per year is 20 percent of the purchase cost.

CHAPTER 12

a. If purchase cost is $2 per unit, what is the EOQ? What is the annual inventory-relevant cost?
b. Suppose that the purchase cost falls to $1.75 per unit for an order size of 500 or more. Now what is the EOQ? What is the annual inventory-relevant cost?
c. What should the company decide for the order size? If the vendor offers more attractive discounts as shown below:

Order less than 500 units, $2 per unit
Order less than 1000 units and more than 499 units, $1.75 per unit
Order more than 999 units, $1.5 per unit

5. A single-period product is priced to sell at $100 per unit, and its cost is $70 per unit. Each unsold unit has a salvage value of $30. Demand is normally distributed with a mean of 1000 units and a standard deviation of 100 units.
   a. How many units should be stocked in order to optimize the profit?
   b. If a 90 percent service level is desired, what should the stock level be?

6. The Supermart Store is about to place an order for Valentine's Day candy. The candy can be bought for $1.40 per box, and it is sold for $2.90 per box up to Valentine's Day. After Valentine's Day, any remaining boxes of candy are sold for $1 per box. All surplus candy can be sold at this reduced price. Demand for the candy at the regular retail price is a random variable with the following discrete probability distribution:

Demand (boxes)	Probability
100	.15
150	.15
180	.15
200	.20
250	.15
300	.10
330	.10

a. Determine the expected demand for boxes of candy at the regular retail price.
b. Determine the optimal number of boxes of candy to stock.
c. If the cost of loss of goodwill, $2.10, is incurred when a potential customer cannot buy a box, what is the optimal number of boxes of candy to stock?

Chapter 13
QUEUING THEORY (QUEUE)

Overview of the QUEUE Decision Support System

This program enables you to analyze several popular queuing problems. These are single-server models with an infinite or a finite queue, with an infinite or a finite population, and with various service-time distributions. Multiple server models can also be analyzed. The program will display the analysis using conventional queuing terminology and performance measures: arrival rate, service rate, utilization rate, average number of customers in the system, average number of customers in the queue, average time a customer spends in the system, average time a customer waits in the queue, and probabilities related to the system status. You may enter a problem from the keyboard or read the problem from a disk(ette).

QUEUE enables you to display, save, modify, and solve your queuing problem. After the model has been solved, the results will be displayed on the screen. By pressing the F8 key, you may copy the output on the screen to the printer.

Special Notes on the QUEUE Program

1. When entering a problem, use the Esc key to reenter the data from the beginning, or the / key to reenter the previous question.

2. The QUEUE program will solve the steady states of the M/M/1, M/M/1 with finite queue, M/M/1 with finite input source, M/G/1, M/D/1, M/M/c, and M/M/c with finite input source queuing problems.

3. When the queuing system has a finite input source, the arrival rate is correspondent to the individual arrival rate, not to the population arrival rate.

4. General distribution means that its standard deviation is known but its distribution pattern is unknown.

Solving Problems with QUEUE

When you first select QUEUE, the function menu, shown in Fig. 13.1, will appear. You can now select the appropriate option. The steps for using QUEUE to solve a queuing problem are listed below:

CHAPTER 13

```
    Welcome to your Queuing Theory (QUEUE) Decision Support System!
           The options available for QUEUE are as follows.
    If you are a first-time user, you might benefit from option 1.

    Option                    Function

       1       ----    Overview of QUEUE Decision Support System
       2       ----    Enter new problem
       3       ----    Read existing problem from disk(ette)
       4       ----    Display and/or print input data
       5       ----    Solve problem
       6       ----    Save problem on disk(ette)
       7       ----    Modify problem
       9       ----    Return to the program menu
       0       ----    Exit from QSB
```

FIGURE 13.1. Function menu of the QUEUE program.

1. Analyze the problem: define queuing parameters.

2. Enter the problem into QSB (use option 2) or read the existing problem from a data disk(ette) (use option 3).

3. Display or print the problem if you want to check and verify data (use option 4).

4. Modify the problem as necessary (use option 7).

5. Solve the problem with display of results (use option 5).

6. Save the problem on a data disk(ette) if you may need it again (use option 6).

7. If you want to solve other problems, go to step 3. Otherwise, return to the program menu (use option 9) to select another program or exit from QSB (use option 0).

Examples

To demonstrate the use of QUEUE, consider the following example problems.

M/M/1 System

A transportation company has a load/unload team to serve its truck fleet. The service time of load/unload is exponentially distributed with a mean of 20 minutes per truck. The trucks arrive at the load/unload area Poisson distributed with a mean of two trucks per hour. Management wants to evaluate the expected performance of the load/unload team. Also, if the team is split into two identical teams which will serve the trucks exponentially distributed with a mean of 40 minutes, what is the effect of this change?

Queuing Theory

Step 1. Analyze the problem and define queuing parameters, such as service rate, arrival rate, and number of servers. The first alternative of the problem is an M/M/1 model with:

Arrival rate = λ = 2 per hour
Service rate = μ = 3 per hour
Number of servers = c = 1

Step 2. Enter the problem (the data underlined in the following figures will be entered into QUEUE):

2.1. Enter problem name and time unit, as shown in Fig. 13.2.

```
Please name your problem using up to 6 characters ? TRUCK
Please specify the time unit (minute, hour, etc.) (default is minute) ? hours
```

FIGURE 13.2. Screen display for entering problem name and time unit.

2.2. Figure 13.3 displays the screen for entering queuing parameters of the problem. Note the conventions that appear on the screen when you enter data.

```
                    QUEUE Model Entry for TRUCK

Please observe the following conventions when entering a problem:
    (1) The Esc key allows you to reenter data from the beginning.
    (2) The  /  key allows you to reenter data for the previous question.
    (3) To enter default value, just press ENTER key.
    (4) Enter 0 arrival rate to return to the function menu.
Customer arrival rate (lambda) per hours ? 2

How many servers (channels) ? 1

Service rate (µ) per hours for one server ? 3

Available service time distributions are:

    1 -- Exponential
    2 -- Constant
    3 -- General

What is the service time distribution (default = 1) ? 1

Is queue finite (Y/N) ? n

Is customer population finite (Y/N) ? n
```

FIGURE 13.3. Screen display for entering the first alternative.

Step 3. You may display or print the entered data, as shown in Fig. 13.4.

123

CHAPTER 13

```
                        M/M/1
Customer arrival rate (lambda)   =   2.000
                 Distribution    :  Poisson
            Number of servers    =   1
        Service rate per server  =   3.000
                 Distribution    :  Poisson
            Mean service time    =   0.333   hours
           Standard deviation    =   0.333   hours
                  Queue limit    =  Infinity
          Customer population    =  Infinity
```

FIGURE 13.4. Screen display of M/M/1 Problem.

Step 4. You have the option to modify the problem as needed. This gives the menu displayed in Fig. 13.5.

```
                    Modify Queuing Data
Select one of the following data for change:
    1 -- Customer arrival rate
    2 -- Number of servers
    3 -- Service rate per server
    4 -- Service time distribution
    5 -- Queue capacity
    6 -- Customer population
    7 -- Display and/or print input data
    0 -- Return to the function menu

Enter the option number ?
```

FIGURE 13.5. Option menu for modifying queuing data.

Step 5. You are now ready to solve the problem. Select option 5 from the function menu. This will call up the question to specify the probability requirement illustrated in Fig. 13.6. The final solution for the first alternative is shown in Fig. 13.7.

```
                   Solving the Model for TRUCK
The probability of n customers in the system is defined as P(n).

Specify the value of n for which P(n) will be evaluated (default=10) ? 10
```

FIGURE 13.6. Screen display for specifying probability calculation.

Step 6. By choosing option 6 from the function menu, you can save the problem on a data disk(ette). Make sure that your data disk(ette) is formatted and inserted in the disk(ette) drive. Figure 13.8 gives the screen display for saving the problem.

Queuing Theory

```
                 Solving the Model for TRUCK


                              M/M/1
With lamda = 2 customers per hours    and µ = 3 customers per hours


                       Utilization factor (p) =  .6666667
    Average number of customers in the system (L) =  2
    Average number of customers in the queue (Lq) =  1.333333
       Average time a customer in the system (W) =  1
       Average time a customer in the queue (Wq) =  .6666666
    The probability that all servers are idle (Po)=  .3333333
    The probability an arriving customer waits(Pw)=  .6666667


P(1) =0.22222  P(2) =0.14815  P(3) =0.09877  P(4) =0.06584  P(5) =0.04390
P(6) =0.02926  P(7) =0.01951  P(8) =0.01301  P(9) =0.00867  P(10) =0.00578


                          10
                          Σ   P(i) =0.655106
                         i=1
```

FIGURE 13.7. M/M/1 solution.

```
              Decide on a file name for saving your problem.
              The file name may be the same as the problem name.
           Type x:xxxxxxxx.xxx for your file name ( e.g., A:XYZ.DAT ).

What is your file name (Type A:, B:, or C: to see all the files) ? a:TRUCK.dat
```

FIGURE 13.8. Screen display for saving a problem.

M/M/2 System

If the transportation company splits the load/unload team into two identical teams with a service rate of 1.5 trucks per hour each, the M/M/2 model can be used to solve this problem. The procedure to enter the data for this alternative is shown in Figs. 13.9 and 13.10, and the solution is displayed in Fig. 13.11.

```
                    QUEUE Model Entry for TRUCK

    Customer arrival rate (lambda) per hour ? 2

    How many servers (channels) ? 2

    Service rate (µ) per hour for one server ? 1.5

    Is customer population finite (Y/N) ? n
```
FIGURE 13.9. Screen display for entering the second alternative.

CHAPTER 13

```
                            M/M/2
    Customer arrival rate (lambda)     =     2.000
                    Distribution       :  Poisson

              Number of servers        =     2
          Service rate per server      =     1.500
                    Distribution       :  Poisson
                Mean service time      =     0.667   hour
              Standard deviation       =     0.667   hour
                     Queue limit       = Infinity
             Customer population       = Infinity
```

FIGURE 13.10. Screen display of M/M/2 problem.

```
                 Solving the Model for TRUCK
                            M/M/2
   With lamda = 2 customers per hour   and μ = 1.5 customers per hour
                         Utilization factor (p) =  .6666667
        Average number of customers in the system (L) =  2.4
        Average number of customers in the queue (Lq) =  1.066667
           Average time a customer in the system (W)  =  1.2
           Average time a customer in the queue (Wq)  =  .5333334
        The probability that all servers are idle (Po)= .2
        The probability an arriving customer waits(Pw)= .5333334

P(1) =0.26667   P(2) =0.17778   P(3) =0.11852   P(4) =0.07901   P(5) =0.05267
P(6) =0.03512   P(7) =0.02341   P(8) =0.01561   P(9) =0.01040   P(10) =0.00694

                          10
                          Σ   P(i) =0.786127
                          i=1
```

FIGURE 13.11. M/M/2 solution.

Exercises

1. Determine the queuing information for the following queuing system:
   Arrival rate = 5 per hour, Poisson distributed
   Number of server = 1
   Service rate = 7 per hour, Poisson distributed
   Number of waiting spaces = 10

2. An M/G/1 queuing system has the following information:
   Arrival rate = 1 per minute
   Service rate = 1.2 per minute
   Standard deviation of service time = 0.9 minute
   a. What is the Lq and Wq for this system?
   b. What is the probability that an arrival customer will need to wait?

Queuing Theory

3. NODE Computer Service, Inc., has four engineers to service its ten mainframes in town. The required service from each mainframe arrives with the mean time of five days exponentially distributed. The expected service time for each service is one day and exponentially distributed. The company considers adding more engineers when the waiting time for each service is expectedly more than half days. Should the company add engineers and, if so, how many?

4. Top Bank wants to build a teller service near a downtown area. The company considers two alternatives. One is to build a booth and hire a clerk. The clerk can serve 30 customers per hour with a Poisson distribution. The other choice is to build an automatic teller machine that can serve almost 30 customers per hour constantly. The clerk is salaried $5 per hour; the machine costs $7 per hour. The customers will arrive at the teller station with a mean of 20 per hour, Poisson distributed. Assume that a waiting customer will cost the company a $4 loss in goodwill. Determine the best choice.

5. A new fast-food restaurant has one cash register in operation. On the average, customers arrive at the register at the rate of 10 per hour. The arrival rate is assumed to follow the Poisson distribution. The cashier takes an average of five minutes with a customer, with a standard deviation of one minute per customer. Assume an arbitrary distribution for service rate.
   a. Determine the average waiting time in the queue.
   b. Assume that the cashier can service customers at a constant rate of six per half hour. What is the average number of customers in the system?
   c. Now assume that the time required to service a customer follows the exponential distribution. The cashier can service six customers per half hour on the average. What is the probability of having less than two customers in the system?

6. Video Games, Inc., owns hundreds of video games that are strategically located at stores and shopping malls throughout Houston. Video game machines break down periodically, and a maintenance worker is dispatched. Broken machines are fixed on a first-come first-served basis. Assume that machines break down at an average rate of one per hour, Poisson distributed. Also assume that a broken machine costs the company $4 per hour (lost sales), and a maintenance worker is salaried at $15 per hour.
   a. Assume that there is only one maintenance worker, and that the average service time is 30 minutes per machine, with a standard deviation of 6 minutes. On the average, how long will a broken machine be inoperable?
   b. Now assume that service time averages 30 minutes and is exponentially distributed. What is the probability of having more than three machines inoperable at one time?
   c. Assume that a second maintenance worker is employed who services machines at the same average rate as the first worker. For both workers, the service time averages 30 minutes and is exponentially distributed. What is the total average hourly cost of this system? Compare with the original one maintenance worker system, which is better?

CHAPTER 13

d. Assume now that the workers work together as a single team so that the average service time is 15 minutes per machine (exponentially distributed). What is the total average cost of this system?

7. The Southern Independent Venders Company (SIV) supplies vended food to a large university. Since, out of anger and frustration, students kick the machines at every opportunity, management has a constant repair problem. Machines break down at an average rate of four per hour, Poisson distributed. Downtime costs an average of $20/machine/hour, and each maintenance worker makes $6 per hour. One worker can service a machine in an average of 12 minutes; two workers together, can service a machine in an average of 10 minutes; three workers together can service a machine in an average of 6 minutes. All service times are exponentially distributed.

a. In the average, how long would a broken machine be out-of-service for each crew size (assume workers work together)?
b. If workers work individually, what will be the out-of-service time for (a)?
c. What is the optimal work crew size and work relationship?

Chapter 14
QUEUING SYSTEM SIMULATION (QSIM)

Overview of the QSIM Decision Support System

This program uses Monte Carlo simulation to analyze queuing systems with up to 20 servers and 20 queues. Queues with up to 100 customers in the line are allowed. The service mechanism is specified by the service time and the form of the distributions. The queuing mechanism is defined by the queue capacity and the priority type. Five forms of distributions are allowed with QSIM when you define service and arrival patterns: the exponential, Erlang, uniform, normal, and constant distributions. The dispatching priority rule may follow FIFO (first in first out), LIFO (last in first out), or random rules. The interarrival time distribution is also specified by one of the five distributions.

Individual servers may be identical or have different characteristics. QSIM allows you to observe changes in the system status as events occur. You can also display or print final statistics. Press the F8 key when you want to print the screen display.

Special Notes on the QSIM Program

1. When entering a problem, use the Esc key to reenter the data from the beginning, or the / key to reenter the previous question.

2. The QSIM program can simulate a single-stage queuing system with up to 20 servers and 20 queues and with different distributions of service and interarrival times.

3. The QSIM program provides the capabilities to specify the total simulation time (default is 100 time units), data collection start time (default is 0), system initial status (default is empty), and random number seed (default is 113). Note that the same random number seed will create the same random number stream.

4. Available distribution patterns for interarrival time and service time are listed in the following sequence:
    a. Exponential
    b. Erlang
    c. Uniform
    d. Normal
    e. Constant

5. The QSIM program enables interactive Monte Carlo discrete event simulation by displaying each event and real-time queuing statistics.

CHAPTER 14

6. Notation

      λ: Mean customer arrival rate
      μ: Mean service rate
 Qmax: maximum queue length
     L: Average number of customers in the system
    Lq: Average number of customers in the queue
    W: Average time a customer spends in the system
   Wq: Average time a customer spends in the queue
   Util: Utilization of a server or servers.

Solving Problems with QSIM

When you first select QSIM, the function menu, shown in Fig. 14.1, will appear. You can now select the appropriate option. The steps for using QSIM to simulate a queuing system are listed below:

```
      Welcome to your Queuing Simulation (QSIM) Decision Support System!
              The options available for QSIM are as follows.
       If you are a first-time user, you might benefit from option 1.

     Option                       Function

       1        ----     Overview of QSIM Decision Support System
       2        ----     Enter new problem
       3        ----     Read existing problem from disk(ette)
       4        ----     Display and/or print input data
       5        ----     Perform simulation
       6        ----     Save problem on disk(ette)
       7        ----     Modify problem
       8        ----     Display and/or print final solution
       9        ----     Return to the program menu
       0        ----     Exit from QSB
```

FIGURE 14.1. Function menu of the QSIM program.

1. Analyze the problem: define queuing parameters.

2. Enter the problem into QSB (use option 2) or read the existing problem from a data disk(ette) (use option 3).

3. Display or print the problem if you want to check and verify data (use option 4).

4. Modify the problem as necessary (use option 7).

5. Simulate the problem by displaying or without displaying discrete events and queuing statistics (use option 5).

Queuing System Simulation

6. Display and print the final solution (use option 8).

7. Save the problem on a data disk(ette) if you may need it again (use option 6).

8. If you want to simulate other problems, go to step 3. Otherwise, return to the program menu (use option 9) to select another program or exit from QSB (use option 0).

Example

To demonstrate the use of QSIM, consider the following example problem. A local bank faces a decision to hire two clerks or lease two automatic teller machines. Table 14.1 shows their service rates and distributions. Customers arrive at the bank Poisson distributed with a mean of 50 per hour. If the two alternatives have the same cost, the manager of the bank wants to know which alternative will have a higher service level, that is, lower customer average waiting time.

Table 14.1. Service rates of the two alternatives

Alternative		Service rate per hour	Distribution
1	Clerk A	35	Poisson
	Clerk B	30	Poisson
2	Machine A	30	Constant
	Machine B	30	Constant

Because of the different service rates of the clerks, you should use Monte Carlo simulation instead of the approximate queuing formula to analyze the problem. The use of QSIM to perform this simulation is as follows:

Step 1. Analyze the problem and define queuing parameters.

Alternative 1:
  Mean interarrival time = $1/\lambda$ = 1/50 hour = 1.2 minutes
  Mean service time for clerk A = $1/\mu$ = 1/35 hour = 1.7143 minutes
  Mean service time for clerk B = $1/\mu$ = 1/30 hour = 2 minutes

Alternative 2:
  Mean interarrival time = 1.2 minutes
  Mean service time for each machine = constant = 2 minutes

Step 2. Enter the problem (the data underlined in the following figures will be entered into QSIM):

2.1. Enter problem name and time unit, as shown in Fig. 14.2.

CHAPTER 14

```
Please name your problem using up to 6 characters ? BANK

Please specify the time unit (second, minute, etc.) (default is minute) ? minute
```

FIGURE 14.2. Screen display for entering problem name and time unit.

2.2. Enter the first alternative into QSIM as shown in Fig. 14.3. Note the conventions that appear on the screen when you enter data.

```
                    QSIM Model Entry for BANK

Please observe the following conventions when entering a problem:
    (1) The Esc  key allows you to reenter data from the beginning.
    (2) The / key allows you to reenter data for the previous question.
    (3) After entering data, the function menu allows you to modify data.

        How many servers (up to 20) ? 2

        Are all servers identical (Y/N) ? n

        Server # 1
            What is the mean service time in minutes ? 1.7143

            Available distributions for service/interarrival time are:

                    1 -- Exponential
                    2 -- Erlang
                    3 -- Uniform
                    4 -- Normal
                    5 -- Constant

            What is the service time distribution (1-5) ? 1

        Server # 2
            What is the mean service time in minutes ? 2

            What is the service time distribution (1-5) ? 1

        How many queues (up to 20, default = 1) ? 1

        What is the queue length limit (≤100, default =100) ?

            Queue dispatching rules are:

                    1 -- FIFO (First In First Out)
                    2 -- LIFO (Last In First Out)
                    3 -- Random
        What is the dispatching rule (1-3) ? 1

        What is the mean interarrival time in minutes ? 1.2

            Available distributions for service/interarrival time are:

                    1 -- Exponential
                    2 -- Erlang
                    3 -- Uniform
                    4 -- Normal
                    5 -- Constant

            What is the interarrival time distribution (1-5) ? 1
```

FIGURE 14.3. Screen display for entering first alternative.

Queuing System Simulation

Step 3. You may display or print the entered data, as shown in Fig. 14.4.

```
                   Input Data Describing Your Problem BANK      page  1
Svr # 1  Mean time:   1.71   Dstn: Expon  Svr # 2  Mean time:   2.00  Dstn: Expon
Qu. # 1  Qu. limit: 100   Dspch: FIFO
Customer mean interarrival time =  1.20   Dstn:  Expon    Random seed = 113
```

FIGURE 14.4. Screen display for first alternative.

Step 4. You have the option of modifying the data as needed. This gives the menu displayed in Fig. 14.5.

```
                Option Menu for Modifying BANK
    Option
        1    ----   Modify service time and distribution
        2    ----   Add one server
        3    ----   Delete one server
        4    ----   Modify queue limit and dispatching rule
        5    ----   Add one queue
        6    ----   Delete one queue
        7    ----   Modify interarrival time and distribution
        8    ----   Display and/or print input data
        9    ----   Return to the function menu
```

FIGURE 14.5. Option menu for modifying a QSIM problem.

Step 5. You are now ready to simulate the problem. Select option 5 from the function menu. This will call up the simulation menu displayed in Fig. 14.6.

```
                  Option Menu for Simulating BANK
     Before performing the simulation, you have the following options,
   which include specifying the simulation time (default = 100) and the
   data collection start time (default = 0), and the system initial
   status (default is empty). You may choose to view each event during
   the process of the simulation. The random seed has a default value
   of 113 unless you choose option 3.

    Option
        1    ----   Specify the simulation and collection times
        2    ----   Specify the system initial status
        3    ----   Specify a new random seed
        4    ----   Simulate and display each event
        5    ----   Simulate without displaying each event
        6    ----   Return to the function menu
```

FIGURE 14.6. Option menu for simulation.

CHAPTER 14

5.1. By selecting option 1, you can specify the simulation time and data collection start time shown in Fig. 14.7.

```
How long do you want to simulate in minutes ? 1000
From what time do you want to collect data ? 0
```

FIGURE 14.7. Screen display for specifying simulation and collection times.

5.2. By selecting option 2, you can specify the initial status of the queuing system, as illustrated in Fig. 14.8.

```
Enter initial number of customers in each queue:
  How many customers are there in queue #  1  ? 0
  Initialization complete.
```

FIGURE 14.8. Screen display for specifying initial status.

5.3. By selecting option 3, you can specify a random number seed for the simulation. For the purpose of comparison, we use the same seed 113 in the two simulations. The entry is shown in Fig. 14.9.

```
Enter random number seed (-32768 to 32767) ? 113
```

FIGURE 14.9. Screen display for specifying random number seed.

5.4. By selecting option 4, you may see the process of simulation. Figure 14.10 shows the initial status of the system, and Figs. 14.11 and 14.15 demonstrate the first five events. The final completion is displayed in Fig. 14.16.

```
              Display the Status for the Queueing System BANK
Time:    0.00 Current event:Initial status Time limit: 1000.00 Data from:    0.0
     No. Servers    Queue    Qmax     Lq        L       Wq       W       Util.
      1   idle       0        0      0.00     0.00    0.00     0.00     0.00000

      2   idle                              0.00     0.00    0.00     0.00     0.00000

     Combined:  Lq =   0.00  L =   0.00  Wq =   0.00  W =   0.00  Util. =  0.0000
                Balking =     0
```

FIGURE 14.10. Screen display of the initial status.

134

Queuing System Simulation

```
            Display the Status for the Queueing System BANK

Time:     1.45 Current event: New arrival   Time limit: 1000.00 Data from:   0.0
No. Servers    Queue    Qmax      Lq        L        Wq       W       Util.
 1   idle        0        0      0.00     0.00      0.00    0.00    0.00000

 2   idle                                 0.00      0.00    0.00    0.00000

Combined: Lq =    0.00  L =    0.00  Wq =    0.00  W =   0.00 Util. =  0.0000
          Balking =     0
```

FIGURE 14.11. Screen display of the first event.

```
            Display the Status for the Queueing System BANK

Time:     2.69 Current event: New arrival   Time limit: 1000.00 Data from:   0.0
No. Servers    Queue    Qmax      Lq        L        Wq       W       Util.
 1   idle        0        0      0.00     0.00      0.00    0.00    0.00000

 2   busy                                 0.46      0.00    1.25    0.45975

Combined: Lq =    0.00  L =    0.46  Wq =    0.00  W =   1.25 Util. =  0.4597
          Balking =     0
```

FIGURE 14.12. Screen display of the second event.

```
            Display the Status for the Queueing System BANK

Time:     2.70 Current event:End-of-service Time limit: 1000.00 Data from:   0.0
No. Servers    Queue    Qmax      Lq        L        Wq       W       Util.
 1   busy        0        0      0.00     0.01      0.00    1.39    0.00670

 2   busy                                 0.46      0.00    1.25    0.46336

Combined: Lq =    0.00  L =    0.47  Wq =    0.00  W =   1.32 Util. =  0.4701
          Balking =     0
```

FIGURE 14.13. Screen display of the third event.

CHAPTER 14

```
              Display the Status for the Queueing System BANK
Time:     2.78 Current event: New arrival   Time limit: 1000.00 Data from:    0.0

No. Servers    Queue    Qmax     Lq        L        Wq         W         Util.

 1   busy        0        0      0.00     0.04      0.00      1.39       0.03531

 2   idle                        0.45     0.00      1.25      0.45002

Combined:  Lq =    0.00  L =   0.49  Wq =   0.00  W =   1.32  Util. =  0.4853
           Balking =    0
```

FIGURE 14.14. Screen display of the fourth event.

```
              Display the Status for the Queueing System BANK
Time:     4.08 Current event:End-of-service Time limit: 1000.00 Data from:    0.0

No. Servers    Queue    Qmax     Lq        L        Wq         W         Util.

 1   busy        0        0      0.00     0.34      0.00      1.39       0.34146

 2   busy                        0.62     0.00      1.74      0.62455

Combined:  Lq =    0.00  L =   0.97  Wq =   0.00  W =   1.62  Util. =  0.9660
           Balking =    0
```

FIGURE 14.15. Screen display of the fifth event.

```
              Display the Status for the Queueing System BANK
Time: 1000.04 Current event:     Finish     Time limit: 1000.00 Data from:    0.0

No. Servers    Queue    Qmax     Lq        L        Wq         W         Util.

 1   idle        0       16      2.65     3.40      3.11      4.94       0.74825

 2   busy                        0.78     3.50      5.46      0.77575

Combined:  Lq =    2.65  L =   4.17  Wq =   3.30  W =   5.20  Util. =  1.5240
           Balking =    0
```

FIGURE 14.16. Screen display of the final event.

Step 6. After the simulation is finished, you may use option 8 in the function menu to display or print the final solution. The menu of options available for displaying or printing is shown in Fig. 14.17. If you choose option 2 from this menu, the final queuing statistics are displayed and automatically printed, as shown in Figs. 14.18 to 14.20. The customer's average waiting time in this case is 3.3 minutes.

136

Queuing System Simulation

```
Option Menu for Displaying and/or Printing the Final Solution to BANK
    You have the following options available for displaying
 or printing the final solution.  If you want to print the
   solution, make sure that the printer is ready.

     Option

        1   ----   Display the final solution only
        2   ----   Display and print the final solution
        3   ----   Return to the function menu
```

FIGURE 14.17. Option menu for displaying and printing QSIM results.

Servers	Util.	Wq.	Var.(Wq)	W.	Var.(W)	Obsvtn.
1	0.7482	3.1063	17.86	4.9403	23.25	408
2	0.7758	3.4975	20.60	5.4616	24.33	395

Summary Results for Servers in BANK   Page : 1

Data collection period: 0 to 1000.04 (in minutes)

FIGURE 14.18. Summary results for servers.

Queues	Qmax.	Qmin.	Current Q	Lq.	Var.(Lq)	L.
1	16	0	0	2.6488	13.98	3.3970

Summary Results for Queues in BANK   Page : 2

Data collection period: 0 to 1000.04 (in minutes)

FIGURE 14.19. Summary results for queues.

```
          Combined Results for BANK     Page : 3

Util.=  1.52400  | Lq.   =2.6488 | V.(Lq)= 13.98 | L.   =4.1728
Wq.  =  3.2987   | V.(Wq)= 19.25 | W.    =5.1967 | V.(W)= 23.85

         Data collection period:  0  to  1000.04  (in minutes )
```

FIGURE 14.20. Combined results.

Step 7. By choosing option 6 from the function menu, you can save the problem on a data disk(ette). Make sure that your data disk(ette) is formatted and inserted in the disk(ette) drive. Figure 14.21 gives the screen display for saving this problem.

CHAPTER 14

```
                  Decide on a file name for saving your problem.
                 The file name may be the same as the problem name.
                Type x:xxxxxxxx.xxx for your file name ( e.g., A:XYZ.DAT ).

What is your file name (Type A:, B:, or C: to see all the files) ? a:BANK.dat
```

FIGURE 14.21. Screen display for saving a problem.

Simulating the Second Configuration

Alternative 2 has the following parameters:

Mean interarrival time = $1/\lambda$ = 1/50 hour = 1.2 minutes
Mean service time = $1/\mu$ = 1/30 hour = 2 minutes for each machine

The procedure to enter the data for this alternative is shown in Figs. 14.22 and 14.23, and the final queuing statistics are shown in Figs. 14.24 to 14.26. The mean waiting time in this case is 1.16 minutes, indicating that the automatic teller machines are the better choice.

```
How many servers (up to 20) ? 2
Are all servers identical (Y/N) ? y
What is the mean service time in minutes ? 2

    Available distributions for service/interarrival time are:

        1 -- Exponential
        2 -- Erlang
        3 -- Uniform
        4 -- Normal
        5 -- Constant

What is the service time distribution (1-5) ? 5
How many queues (up to 20, default = 1) ? 1
What is the queue length limit (≤100, default =100) ? 100

    Queue dispatching rules are:

        1 -- FIFO (First In First Out)
        2 -- LIFO (Last In First Out)
        3 -- Random

What is the dispatching rule (1-3) ? 1

What is the mean interarrival time in minutes ? 1.2

    Available distributions for service/interarrival time are:

        1 -- Exponential
        2 -- Erlang
        3 -- Uniform
        4 -- Normal
        5 -- Constant

What is the interarrival time distribution (1-5) ? 1
```

FIGURE 14.22. Screen display for entering the second alternative.

Queuing System Simulation

```
              Input Data Describing Your Problem BANK      page  1
Svr # 1  Mean time:  2.00  Dstn: Const | Svr # 2  Mean time:  2.00  Dstn: Const
Qu. # 1  Qu. limit: 100  Dspch: FIFO
Customer mean interarrival time =  1.20   Dstn:  Expon    Random seed = 113
```

FIGURE 14.23. Screen display for the second alternative.

```
              Summary Results for Servers in BANK    Page : 1
Servers |  Util. |   Wq.  | Var.(Wq) |   W.   | Var.(W) | Obsvtn.
   1    | 0.7755 | 1.1119 | 1.9805   | 3.1119 | 1.9805  |  388
   2    | 0.7894 | 1.1986 | 2.1011   | 3.1986 | 2.1011  |  395
       Data collection period:  0  to  1000.698  (in minutes )
```

FIGURE 14.24. Summary results of servers for the second alternative.

```
              Summary Results for Queues in BANK    Page : 2
Queues | Qmax. | Qmin. | Current Q |  Lq.   | Var.(Lq) |   L.
   1   |  10   |   0   |    0      | 0.9043 |  1.9107  | 1.6797
       Data collection period:  0  to  1000.698  (in minutes )
```

FIGURE 14.25. Summary results of queues for the second alternative.

```
              Combined Results for BANK       Page : 3
Util.= 1.56491 | Lq.    =0.9043 | V.(Lq)=1.9107 | L.    =2.4692
Wq.  = 1.1557  | V.(Wq) =2.0432 | W.    =3.1557 | V.(W) =2.0432
       Data collection period:  0  to  1000.698  (in minutes )
```

FIGURE 14.26. Combined results for the second alternative.

Exercises

1. Compare the following three queuing systems. Assume that the mean interarrival time is 8 minutes and the mean service time is 10 minutes:
   a. M/M/2 system (solvable by QUEUE program).
   b. Two servers, uniform service time from 8 minutes to 12 minutes, and exponential interarrival time.
   c. M/D/2 system.
   Simulate up to 2000 minutes.

CHAPTER 14

2. Compare the following M/M/1 queuing systems, assuming that the mean interarrival time = 15 minutes and mean service time = 10 minutes:
   a. Dispatching is FIFO (solvable by QUEUE).
   b. Dispatching is LIFO.
   c. Dispatching is random.
   Simulate up to 2000 minutes.

3. Compare the following three server systems, assuming that the mean interarrival time = 2 minutes and the mean service time = 5 minutes:
   a. M/M/3 (Solvable by QUEUE).
   b. Interarrival time with standard deviation of 1 minute; service time exponentially distributed.
   c. Interarrival time is normal with standard deviation of 1 minute and constant service time.
   d. Interarrival time and service time are constant.
   Simulate up to 10 hours.

4. Buck Stadium has ten clerks and ten automatic machines to sell tickets for the upcoming football season. Each clerk can sell 60 tickets per hour with a Poisson distribution, and each machine can sell 55 tickets per hour constantly. In general, jockeying is allowed. What is the expected length of time before each server when you buy a ticket? Assume there are 20 lines and the arrival rate is 100 per hour, Poisson distributed. Simulate up to 10 hours.

5. A supercomputer system has four processors. According to their configuration, each processor can process jobs at different speeds. Expected process time for incoming jobs on each processor are 10, 12, 13, and 15 seconds, respectively. Assume that the process times are exponentially distributed. The jobs arrive at the system with mean of 10 per minute Poisson distributed.
   a. If there is only one queue and the system applies the FIFO rule, what is the expected number of jobs in the queue? How long does each job stay in the system?
   b. Do part (a) if the system applies the LIFO rule. Simulate up to 100 minutes.

Chapter 15
DECISION AND PROBABILITY THEORY (DSPB)

Overview of the DSPB Decision Support System

This program provides four capabilities: mean and variance analysis, Bayesian analysis, payoff table analysis, and decision tree analysis. With the mean and variance analysis, after you enter up to 100 outcomes and probabilities, the program will display the mean and variance of the sample. With the Bayesian analysis, you provide the prior probabilities of the states of nature and the conditional probabilities of the outcomes; the program can then compute the joint probabilities, marginal probabilities, and posterior probabilities. With the payoff table analysis, DSPB requires you to provide a payoff table with up to 40 states of nature and 40 alternatives, and the program will display decisions under different criteria.

The decision tree analysis requires that you provide a tree with at the most 80 branches. The branches and nodes should be numbered sequentially from 1 following the precedence relationships of the branches. Each branch is specified by alternative or probability. A node is a chance node, a decision node, or an end node. Any time you want a copy of the output on the screen, press the F8 key.

Special Notes on the DSPB Program

1. When entering a problem, use the BACKSPACE key to move the cursor to the position where you want to make a correction.

2. The DSPB contains the mean and variance calculations for a sample, the Bayesian probability calculation, the payoff table analysis, and the decision tree analysis.

3. There are six different criteria you may choose when analyzing payoff tables: maximin, maximax, minimax regret, expected value, principle of insufficient reason, and expected regret.

4. The states of nature and alternatives are automatically named by S1, S2, ..., Sn and A1, A2, ..., An.

5. The decision tree is entered based on the branch. The nodes should be numbered sequentially beginning with 1. The start node of each branch should be numbered lower than the end node. Each node can be a decision node or a chance node. When entering a decision tree, the decision node is represented by 1, and the chance node is represented by 2.

6. When entering a decision tree into DSPB, all the termination nodes should also be numbered.

Solving Problems with DSPB

When you first select DSPB, the function menu, shown in Fig. 15.1, will appear. You can now select the appropriate option. The steps for using DSPB to solve a related probability or decision problem are listed below:

```
Welcome to your Decision/Probability Theory (DSPB) Decision Support System!
          The options available for DSPB are as follows.
     If you are a first-time user, you might benefit from option 1.

        Option                  Function

          1        ----    Overview of DSPB Decision Support System
          2        ----    Enter new problem
          3        ----    Read existing problem from disk(ette)
          4        ----    Display and/or print input data
          5        ----    Solve problem
          6        ----    Save problem on disk(ette)
          7        ----    Modify problem
          9        ----    Return to the program menu
          0        ----    Exit from QSB
```

FIGURE 15.1. Function menu of the DSPB program.

1. Analyze the problem: prepare the data or decision tree.

2. Enter the problem into QSB (use option 2) or read the existing problem from a data disk(ette) (use option 3).

3. Display or print the problem if you want to check and verify data (use option 4).

4. Modify the problem as necessary (use option 7).

5. Solve the problem with display of results (use option 5).

6. Save the problem on a data disk(ette) if you may need it again (use option 6).

7. If you want to solve other problems, go to step 3. Otherwise, return to the program menu (use option 9) to select another program or exit from QSB (use option 0).

Examples

To demonstrate the use of DSPB, consider the following example problems.

Decision and Probability Theory

Mean and Variance

The scores on an examination are listed in Table 15.1. What is the average and standard deviation of the scores on this examination?

Table 15.1. Results of an examination

Student	Score	Student	Score
1	60	16	71
2	75	17	94
3	98	18	98
4	79	19	69
5	86	20	78
6	97	21	83
7	100	22	89
8	67	23	90
9	75	24	82
10	85	25	96
11	92	26	93
12	96	27	91
13	87	28	85
14	85	29	77
15	84	30	96

Step 1. Analyze and prepare data for entry. The current problem has 30 observations.

Step 2. Enter the problem (the data underlined in the following figures will be entered into DSPB):

2.1. Enter problem name SCORE.

2.2. Select one of the four options shown in Fig. 15.2 to specify your problem. Note the conventions that appear on the screen when you enter data.

```
              DSPB Model Entry for SCORE
Please observe the following conventions when entering a problem:

(1) Select one of the following options for entering your problem.
(2) Then enter data for your problem.
(3) After you enter your data press the ENTER key.
(4) On the same data entry page, you may correct errors by pressing
    the BACKSPACE key to move the cursor to the correct position.
(5) When you are satisfied with the data on a page, press the SPACE BAR.
(6) To enter the default value, just press the ENTER key.
```

FIGURE 15.2. Screen display of DSPB for selecting problems.

CHAPTER 15

```
Select one of the options for entering your problem:

    1 -- Mean and variance analysis
    2 -- Bayesian analysis
    3 -- Payoff table analysis
    4 -- Decision tree
    0 -- Return to the function menu

    Please enter the option number ? 1
```

FIGURE 15.2 *(cont.)* Screen display of DSPB for selecting problems.

2.3. Figure 15.3 displays the screen for defining the number of observations in the sample.

```
        Enter Data for Mean and Variance Analysis

        You may enter up to 100 observations.
             How many observations ? 30
```

FIGURE 15.3. Screen display for entering number of observations.

2.4. Figure 15.4 displays the screen for entering observations and probabilities. Note that if you do not assign a probability to an observation, DSPB will automatically assign an equal probability to any unassigned observations.

```
           Enter Data for Mean and Variance Analysis

Observation  Probability    Observation  Probability    Observation  Probability

 1 <60    > <    >      11 <92    > <    >      21 <83    > <    >
 2 <75    > <    >      12 <96    > <    >      22 <89    > <    >
 3 <98    > <    >      13 <87    > <    >      23 <90    > <    >
 4 <79    > <    >      14 <85    > <    >      24 <82    > <    >
 5 <86    > <    >      15 <84    > <    >      25 <96    > <    >
 6 <97    > <    >      16 <71    > <    >      26 <93    > <    >
 7 <100   > <    >      17 <94    > <    >      27 <91    > <    >
 8 <67    > <    >      18 <98    > <    >      28 <85    > <    >
 9 <75    > <    >      19 <69    > <    >      29 <77    > <    >
10 <85    > <    >      20 <78    > <    >      30 <96    > <    >
```

FIGURE 15.4. Screen display for entering observations.

Step 3. You may display or print the entered data, as shown in Fig. 15.5.

Decision and Probability Theory

```
Input Data Describing Your Problem SCORE -- Mean and Variance Analysis
    Page 1
Observation   Probability    Observation   Probability    Observation   Probability

 1  <60   >   <0.0333>       11  <92   >   <0.0333>       21  <83   >   <0.0333>
 2  <75   >   <0.0333>       12  <96   >   <0.0333>       22  <89   >   <0.0333>
 3  <98   >   <0.0333>       13  <87   >   <0.0333>       23  <90   >   <0.0333>
 4  <79   >   <0.0333>       14  <85   >   <0.0333>       24  <82   >   <0.0333>
 5  <86   >   <0.0333>       15  <84   >   <0.0333>       25  <96   >   <0.0333>
 6  <97   >   <0.0333>       16  <71   >   <0.0333>       26  <93   >   <0.0333>
 7  <100  >   <0.0333>       17  <94   >   <0.0333>       27  <91   >   <0.0333>
 8  <67   >   <0.0333>       18  <98   >   <0.0333>       28  <85   >   <0.0333>
 9  <75   >   <0.0333>       19  <69   >   <0.0333>       29  <77   >   <0.0333>
10  <85   >   <0.0333>       20  <78   >   <0.0333>       30  <96   >   <0.0333>
```

FIGURE 15.5. Screen display of observations.

Step 4. You have the option of modifying the problem as needed. This gives the menu displayed in Fig. 15.6.

```
              Option Menu for Modifying SCORE
    Option
       1  ----  Modify the mean and variance analysis data
       2  ----  Modify the Bayesian analysis data
       3  ----  Modify the payoff table
       4  ----  Modify the decision tree
       5  ----  Display and/or print input data
       6  ----  Return to the function menu
```

FIGURE 15.6. Option menu for modifying a problem.

Step 5. You are now ready to solve the problem. Select option 5 from the function menu. This will call up the mean and variance analysis in Fig. 15.7.

```
         Mean and Variance Analysis for SCORE
             Number of observations  :  30
             Mean of the sample      :  85.26666
             Variance of the sample  :  103.5981
             Standard deviation      :  10.17832
```

FIGURE 15.7. Mean and variance for the examination.

Step 6. By choosing option 6 from the function menu, you can save the problem on a data disk(ette). Make sure that your data disk(ette) is formatted and inserted in the disk(ette) drive. Figure 15.8 gives the screen display for saving your problem.

145

CHAPTER 15

```
                Decide on a file name for saving your problem.
                The file name may be the same as the problem name.
                Type x:xxxxxxxx.xxx for your file name ( e.g., A:XYZ.DAT ).

What is your file name (Type A:, B:, or C: to see all the files) ? a:SCORE.dat
```

FIGURE 15.8. Screen display for saving the score problem.

Bayesian Analysis

The following example demonstrates the process of Bayesian analysis using DSPB. Given the prior probabilities of the states of nature (Table 15.2) and the conditional probabilities of alternatives (Table 15.3), find the posterior (revised) probabilities of the states of nature.

Table 15.2. Prior probabilities of the states of nature

State of nature	Probability
S1	0.3
S2	0.4
S3	0.3

Table 15.3. Conditional probabilities of alternatives

	States of nature		
Alternative	S1	S2	S3
A1	.1	.6	.4
A2	.2	.3	.1
A3	.5	.1	.4
A4	.2	0	.1

The procedure to enter the data for this problem is shown in Figs. 15.9 to 15.12, and the solution process by selecting option 5 in the function menu is shown in Figs. 15.13 to 15.17.

Payoff Table Analysis

The following example shows the procedure for a payoff table analysis using DSPB. In a decision situation, a manager faces the choices shown in Table 15.4:

Table 15.4. Payoff in profit

	States of nature			
Alternative	S1	S2	S3	S4
A1	300	50	500	1000
A2	−200	1000	1200	200
A3	500	600	350	−50
A4	200	1500	−500	400

Decision and Probability Theory

Suppose the probabilities of the states of nature S1 to S4 are 0.2, 0.3, 0.1, and 0.4, respectively. What is the decision when using the following criteria?

1. Maximin
2. Minimax regret
3. Expected value
4. Principle of insufficient reason

Using DSPB, the data entry is shown in Figs. 15.18 to 15.21, and the solution process is shown in Figs. 15.22 to 15.29.

```
                DSPB Model Entry for BAYESN

    Please observe the following conventions when entering a problem:

    (1) Select one of the following options for entering your problem.
    (2) Then enter data for your problem.
    (3) After you enter your data press the ENTER key.
    (4) On the same data entry page, you may correct errors by pressing
        the BACKSPACE key to move the cursor to the correct position.
    (5) When you are satisfied with the data on a page, press the SPACE BAR.
    (6) To enter the default value, just press the ENTER key.

    Select one of the options for entering your problem:

        1 -- Mean and variance analysis
        2 -- Bayesian analysis
        3 -- Payoff table analysis
        4 -- Decision tree
        0 -- Return to the function menu

        Please enter the option number ? 2
```

FIGURE 15.9. Screen display of DSPB for selecting Bayesian analysis.

```
                Enter Data for Bayesian Analysis

        You may enter up to 40 states of nature and 40 alternatives.
        The states of nature will be named S1,S2,...,Sn, and the
        alternatives will be named A1,A2,...,An.

            How many states of nature(0 to return) ? 3

            How many alternatives (0 to return) ? 4
```

FIGURE 15.10. Screen display for entering numbers of states/alternatives.

```
    Enter Data for Bayesian Analysis--Prior Probabilities for States of Nature

    S1:  .3_____    S2:  .4_____    S3:  .3_____
```

FIGURE 15.11. Screen display for entering prior probabilities.

CHAPTER 15

```
         Enter Data for Bayesian Analysis--Conditional Probabilities Pg 1

State    Alternative
S1       A1:  .1_____  A2:  .2_____  A3:  .5_____  A4:  .2_____
S2       A1:  .6_____  A2:  .3_____  A3:  .1_____  A4:  .0_____
S3       A1:  .4_____  A2:  .1_____  A3:  .4_____  A4:  .1_____
```

FIGURE 15.12. Screen display for entering conditional probabilities.

```
         Bayesian Analysis--Prior Probabilities for States of Nature

S1:  0.300000    S2:  0.400000    S3:  0.300000
```

FIGURE 15.13. Screen display of the prior probabilities.

```
              Bayesian Analysis--Conditional Probabilities Pg 1

State    Alternative
S1       A1:  0.100000 A2:  0.200000 A3:  0.500000 A4:  0.200000
S2       A1:  0.600000 A2:  0.300000 A3:  0.100000 A4:         0
S3       A1:  0.400000 A2:  0.100000 A3:  0.400000 A4:  0.100000
```

FIGURE 15.14. Screen display of the conditional probabilities.

```
                 Bayesian Analysis--Joint Probabilities Pg 1

State    Alternative
S1       A1:  0.030000 A2:  0.060000 A3:  0.150000 A4:  0.060000
S2       A1:  0.240000 A2:  0.120000 A3:  0.040000 A4:  0.000000
S3       A1:  0.120000 A2:  0.030000 A3:  0.120000 A4:  0.030000
```

FIGURE 15.15. Screen display of the joint probabilities.

```
          Bayesian Analysis--Marginal Probabilities for Alternatives

A1:  0.390000   A2:  0.210000   A3:  0.310000   A4:  0.090000
```

FIGURE 15.16. Screen display of the marginal probabilities.

```
         Bayesian Analysis--Posterior or Revised Probabilities Pg 1

State    Alternative
S1       A1:  0.076923 A2:  0.285714 A3:  0.483871 A4:  0.666667
S2       A1:  0.615385 A2:  0.571429 A3:  0.129032 A4:  0.000000
S3       A1:  0.307692 A2:  0.142857 A3:  0.387097 A4:  0.333333
```

FIGURE 15.17. Screen display of the posterior probabilities.

Decision and Probability Theory

```
                DSPB Model Entry for PAYOFF

Please observe the following conventions when entering a problem:

(1) Select one of the following options for entering your problem.
(2) Then enter data for your problem.
(3) After you enter your data press the ENTER key.
(4) On the same data entry page, you may correct errors by pressing
    the BACKSPACE key to move the cursor to the correct position.
(5) When you are satisfied with the data on a page, press the SPACE BAR.
(6) To enter the default value, just press the ENTER key.


Select one of the options for entering your problem:

    1 -- Mean and variance analysis
    2 -- Bayesian analysis
    3 -- Payoff table analysis
    4 -- Decision tree
    0 -- Return to the function menu

    Please enter the option number ? 3
```

FIGURE 15.18. Screen display of DSPB for selecting payoff table analysis.

```
            Enter Data for Payoff Table Analysis

    You may enter up to 40 states of nature and 40 alternatives.
    The states of nature will be named S1,S2,...,Sn, and the
    alternatives will be named A1,A2,...,An.

            How many states of nature(0 to return) ? 4

            How many alternatives (0 to return) ? 4

            Payoff represents: 1--profit, 2--cost  ? 1
```

FIGURE 15.19. Screen display for defining payoff table.

```
Enter Data for Payoff Table Analysis--Probabilities for States of Nature

S1:  .2_____   S2:  .3_____   S3:  .1_____   S4:  .4_____
```

FIGURE 15.20. Screen display for entering probability of state of nature.

```
        Enter Data for Payoff Table Analysis--Payoff Values Pg 1

State   Alternative
S1      A1: 300_____  A2: -200____  A3: 500_____  A4: 200_____
S2      A1: 50_____  A2: 1000____  A3: 600_____  A4: 1500____
S3      A1: 500_____  A2: 1200____  A3: 350_____  A4: -500____
S4      A1: 1000____  A2: 200_____  A3: -50_____  A4: 400_____
```

FIGURE 15.21. Screen display for entering payoff values.

CHAPTER 15

```
              Payoff Table Analysis

Select one of the following criteria:

        1 -- Maximin
        2 -- Maximax
        3 -- Minimax regret
        4 -- Expected value
        5 -- Principle of insufficient reason
        6 -- Expected regret
        9 -- Return to the function menu

What is your decision criterion  ? 1
```

FIGURE 15.22. Screen display for selecting criterion—maximin.

```
              Payoff Table Analysis

      Your decision criterion : Maximin

        The decision will be : A1

              Maximin =  50
```

FIGURE 15.23. Screen display of payoff analysis—maximin.

```
              Payoff Table Analysis

Select one of the following criteria:

        1 -- Maximin
        2 -- Maximax
        3 -- Minimax regret
        4 -- Expected value
        5 -- Principle of insufficient reason
        6 -- Expected regret
        9 -- Return to the function menu

What is your decision criterion  ? 3
```

FIGURE 15.24. Screen display for selecting criterion—minimax regret.

```
              Payoff Table Analysis

    Your decision criterion : Minimax regret

        The decision will be : A2

           Minimax regret =  800
```

FIGURE 15.25. Screen display of payoff analysis—minimax regret.

Decision and Probability Theory

```
              Payoff Table Analysis
    Select one of the following criteria:
        1 -- Maximin
        2 -- Maximax
        3 -- Minimax regret
        4 -- Expected value
        5 -- Principle of insufficient reason
        6 -- Expected regret
        9 -- Return to the function menu
    What is your decision criterion   ? 4
```

FIGURE 15.26. Screen display for selecting criterion—expected value.

```
              Payoff Table Analysis
    Your decision criterion : Expected value

          The decision will be : A4

            Expected value =  600
```

FIGURE 15.27. Screen display of payoff analysis—expected value.

```
    Select one of the following criteria:
        1 -- Maximin
        2 -- Maximax
        3 -- Minimax regret
        4 -- Expected value
        5 -- Principle of insufficient reason
        6 -- Expected regret
        9 -- Return to the function menu
    What is your decision criterion   ? 5
```

FIGURE 15.28. Screen display for selecting criterion—insufficient reason.

```
              Payoff Table Analysis
    Your decision criterion : Principle of insufficient reason

          The decision will be : A2

            Expected value =  550
```

FIGURE 15.29. Screen display of payoff analysis—insufficient reason.

Decision Tree

The following example illustrates the solution of a decision tree using DSPB. An oil drilling decision situation is shown in the decision tree in Fig. 15.30. Assume that the final outcomes represent profits, and the amounts in parentheses associated with decision branches are costs. Make the decision that will maximize the expected profit.

CHAPTER 15

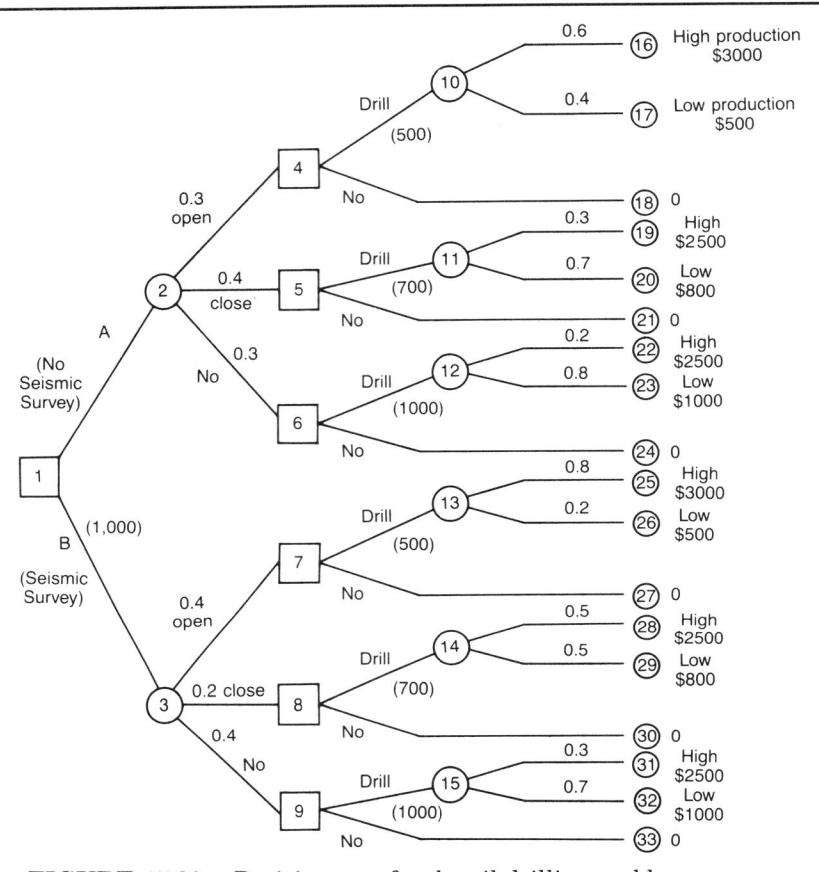

FIGURE 15.30. Decision tree for the oil drilling problem.

Using DSPB to solve this decision tree, Figs. 15.31 to 15.34 display the procedure for data entry, and Fig. 15.35 shows the decision analysis for each node on the tree.

```
                    DSPB Model Entry for DTREE

Please observe the following conventions when entering a problem:

(1) Select one of the following options for entering your problem.
(2) Then enter data for your problem.
(3) After you enter your data press the ENTER key.
(4) On the same data entry page, you may correct errors by pressing
    the BACKSPACE key to move the cursor to the correct position.
(5) When you are satisfied with the data on a page, press the SPACE BAR.
(6) To enter the default value, just press the ENTER key.
Select one of the options for entering your problem:
```

FIGURE 15.31. Screen display of DSPB selecting decision tree analysis.

Decision and Probability Theory

```
1 -- Mean and variance analysis
2 -- Bayesian analysis
3 -- Payoff table analysis
4 -- Decision tree
0 -- Return to the function menu

Please enter the option number ? 4
```

FIGURE 15.31 *(cont.)* Screen display of DSPB selecting decision tree analysis.

```
        Enter Data for Decision Tree Analysis


Before entering data, you have to prepare a decision tree with
numbered nodes and numbered branches. The program can solve
decision trees with up to 80 branches. The nodes and branches
should be numbered sequentially from 1. The number of the start
node should be lower than the number of the end node for every
branch.  Each node can be either a decision node or a chance
node represented by 1 or 2, respectively. For each branch, you
may have probability, payoff/cost value, and name with it.  The
following data entry is performed branch by branch.


  How many branches are there in your decision tree ? 32

Do you want to maximize (1) or minimize (2) criterion? (Enter 1 or 2)? 1
```

FIGURE 15.32. Screen display for defining a decision tree.

```
         Enter Data for Decision Tree Analysis Page 1
```

Branch number	Branch name	Start node	End node	Start node type	Probability	Payoff/cost
1	<A(No se.)>	<1>	<2>	<1>	<>	<>
2	<B(Ses.)>	<1>	<3>	<1>	<>	<-1000>
3	<Open>	<2>	<4>	<2>	<.3>	<>
4	<Close>	<2>	<5>	<2>	<.4>	<>
5	<No>	<2>	<6>	<2>	<.3>	<>
6	<Open>	<3>	<7>	<2>	<.4>	<>
7	<Close>	<3>	<8>	<2>	<.2>	<>
8	<No>	<3>	<9>	<2>	<.4>	<>
9	<Drill>	<4>	<10>	<1>	<>	<-500>
10	<No drill>	<4>	<18>	<1>	<>	<>
11	<Drill>	<5>	<11>	<1>	<>	<-700>
12	<No drill>	<5>	<21>	<1>	<>	<>
13	<Drill>	<6>	<12>	<1>	<>	<-1000>
14	<No drill>	<6>	<24>	<1>	<>	<>
15	<Drill>	<7>	<13>	<1>	<>	<-500>
16	<No drill>	<7>	<27>	<1>	<>	<>
17	<Drill>	<8>	<14>	<1>	<>	<-700>
18	<No drill>	<8>	<30>	<1>	<>	<>
19	<Drill>	<9>	<15>	<1>	<>	<-1000>
20	<No drill>	<9>	<33>	<1>	<>	<>

FIGURE 15.33. Screen display for entering a decision tree.

CHAPTER 15

Enter Data for Decision Tree Analysis Page 2

Branch number	Branch name	Start node	End node	Start node type	Probability	Payoff/cost
21	<High >	<10 >	<16 >	<2 >	<.6 >	<3000 >
22	<Low >	<10 >	<17 >	<2 >	<.4 >	<500 >
23	<High >	<11 >	<19 >	<2 >	<.3 >	<2500 >
24	<Low >	<11 >	<20 >	<2 >	<.7 >	<800 >
25	<High >	<12 >	<22 >	<2 >	<.2 >	<2500 >
26	<Low >	<12 >	<23 >	<2 >	<.8 >	<1000 >
27	<High >	<13 >	<25 >	<2 >	<.8 >	<3000 >
28	<Low >	<13 >	<26 >	<2 >	<.2 >	<500 >
29	<High >	<14 >	<28 >	<2 >	<.5 >	<2500 >
30	<Low >	<14 >	<29 >	<2 >	<.5 >	<800 >
31	<High >	<15 >	<31 >	<2 >	<.3 >	<2500 >
32	<Low >	<15 >	<32 >	<2 >	<.7 >	<1000 >

FIGURE 15.34. Screen display for entering a decision tree (continued).

Decision Tree Analysis

The following analysis will display the expected value
and decision (if a decision node) on each node

Decision Tree Analysis

Node	Type of node	Expected value	Decision
1	decision	784.0001	A(Nose.
2	chance	784.0001	
3	chance	1170	
4	decision	1500	Drill
5	decision	610	Drill
6	decision	300	Drill
7	decision	2000	Drill
8	decision	950	Drill
9	decision	450	Drill
10	chance	2000	
11	chance	1310	
12	chance	1300	
13	chance	2500	
14	chance	1650	
15	chance	1450	

FIGURE 15.35. Screen display for decision tree analysis.

Decision and Probability Theory

Exercises

1. Find the mean and variance for the following data:

Data	Probability
5	.01
11	.10
90	.09
23	.23
35	.27
19	.15
15	.02
42	.06
55	.03
68	.04

2. The following matrix gives the posterior probabilities for three states of nature (A, B, and C) and three survey results (a, b, and c).

		States of nature		
		A	B	C
Survey results	a	.67	.12	.21
	b	.07	.77	.16
	c	.04	.07	.89

The marginal probabilities associated with a, b, and c are .24, .31, and .45, respectively.

a. Determine the joint probabilities associated with each survey result and state of nature.

b. What are the conditional probabilities, that is, the probabilities of each survey result under the conditions of each state of nature?

3. Consider the following profit table, where I to V are alternatives and S1 to S5 are states of nature. The prior probabilities associated with S1 to S5 are .3, .2, .1, .15, and .25, respectively.

		Alternatives				
		I	II	III	IV	V
States of nature	S1	10000	17000	5000	35000	45000
	S2	31000	67000	45000	19000	51000
	S3	11000	13000	13000	9000	8000
	S4	39000	22000	18000	29000	40000
	S5	54000	43000	32000	35000	45000

CHAPTER 15

a. Which alternative maximizes expected monetary value?
b. Which is the best decision if you use minimax regret as the criterion?
c. What if you use maximin as the criterion?

4. The following payoff matrix indicates the monetary values that would be realized for each of the three alternatives (A1, A2, A3) and the three states of nature (S1, S2, S3). All dollar amounts are in thousands.

Prob.		A1	A2	A3
.3	S1	$1000	0	− 400
.5	S2	− 100	0	100
.2	S3	− 2000	0	500

a. Use the expected value to choose an alternative.
b. A market analyst offers to conduct a survey to determine which state of nature might occur. The analyst indicates that the survey will be 80 percent accurate—that is, if S1 will occur, then there is an 80 percent chance that the survey will indicate this, while there is a 10 percent chance that it will indicate each of the other two states. The same is true if S2 occurs or if S3 occurs. If you survey, then either A1 or A3 must be chosen.
  (1) Determine the posterior probabilities.
  (2) Draw a decision tree to represent these situations and find the best strategy.

5. The following questions relate to the attached decision tree. Note that the cost of the survey has not been substracted from the terminal values. The survey costs $100.
a. What is the recommended strategy?
b. What is the most you would be willing to pay for the survey information?

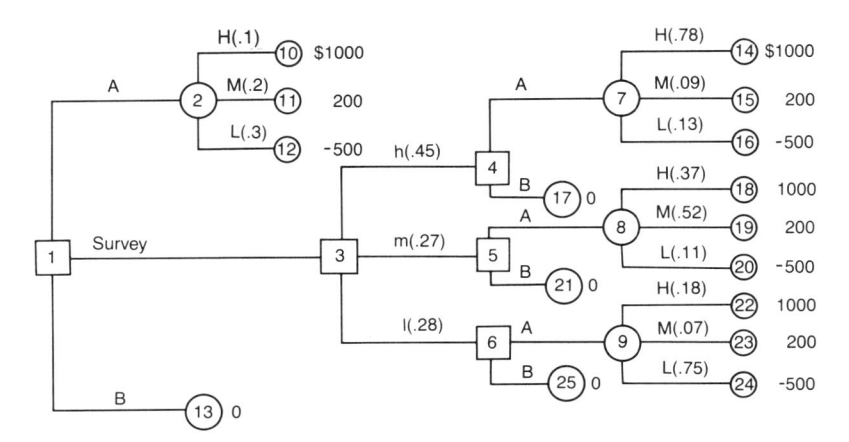

6. Joe Stingy needed a camera. The model that appealed to him had a firm retail price of $420 at local camera stores. On the chance that he could save some money, Joe called on Slippery Jim, the proprietor of a discount store that specialized in "seconds"—articles that had been rejected for retail sale. Sure enough, Slippery Jim had just the camera Joe wanted, and he was offering it for $270. Looking it over, Joe thought the camera body seemed fine but that the lens was questionable. From experience, he felt there was a .3 probability that the lens would not be acceptable. A new lens would cost $240. After buying the camera from Slippery Jim, Joe might find the lens was not acceptable, and a new lens would have to be purchased at this price. Fortunately, testing services were available. Joe had a "friend" who could tell for certain whether the lens was acceptable or not, but he charged $20 for the service. On the other hand, a local lens testing service charged only $12, but the probability that the testing would be correct (whether the lens was acceptable or not) was .9. Slippery Jim would allow Joe to test the camera only if he deposited $10 toward its purchase. The $10 would be forfeited if Joe decided not to buy the camera after testing.
   a. Assume that Joe will not use the testing services. That is, he will make a decision immediately. Construct the payoff table that describes the alternatives, states of nature, and associated monetary values. What is the decision by expected value?
   b. Now assume that Joe either decides immediately, or he uses the testing services. Construct a decision tree that describes the sequence of alternatives available to Joe and analyze it to determine the best decision for Joe.

Chapter 16
MARKOV PROCESS (MKV)

Overview of the MKV Decision Support System

This program enables you to find the probability of a system in a particular state at a particular time period by using the Markov process model. The inputs of the program include the initial state probability vector and the transition probability matrix. The maximum number of states allowed in this program is 50. If the initial state probabilities are unknown, the program will assume equal probability for each state. The program allows you to define names of states with up to six characters. The default names are S1, S2, . . ., Sn. You may save data on or read data from a disk(ette).

You have the option of displaying every state probability at each period. The approximate steady state probabilities will be shown when the differences of all the probabilities of the same state between two consecutive periods are less than 1.0E-6. You can also specify the number of periods, and the program will stop at that period. The maximum number of periods is 32000. Any time you want a copy of the output on the screen, press the F8 key.

Special Notes on the MKV Program

1. When entering a problem, use the BACKSPACE key to move the cursor back to the position where you want to make corrections.

2. The MKV program solves for steady state by assuming that the process is a Markov process. Steady state is attained when the differences of the state probabilities between two consecutive periods are less than 1.0E-6.

3. You may specify the maximum number of iterations for the MKV program to proceed with the Markov process.

4. The recurrent period for each state will be displayed after the steady state has been found.

Solving Problems with MKV

When you first select MKV, the function menu, shown in Fig. 16.1, will appear. You can now select the appropriate option. The steps for using MKV to perform a Markov process are listed below:

Markov Process

```
    Welcome to your Markov Process (MKV) Decision Support System!
          The options available for MKV are as follows.
    If you are a first-time user, you might benefit from option 1.

    Option                  Function

       1        ----    Overview of MKV Decision Support System
       2        ----    Enter new problem
       3        ----    Read existing problem from disk(ette)
       4        ----    Display and/or print input data
       5        ----    Solve problem
       6        ----    Save problem on disk(ette)
       7        ----    Modify problem
       8        ----    Display and/or print final solution
       9        ----    Return to the program menu
       0        ----    Exit from QSB
```

FIGURE 16.1. Function menu of the MKV program.

1. Analyze the problem: prepare state probabilities.

2. Enter the problem into QSB (use option 2) or read the existing problem from a data disk(ette) (use option 3).

3. Display or print the problem if you want to check and verify data (use option 4).

4. Modify the problem as necessary (use option 7).

5. Perform the Markov process by displaying or without displaying steps (use option 5).

6. Display and print the final solution (use option 8).

7. Save the problem on a data disk(ette) if you may need it again (use option 6).

8. If you want to solve other problems, go to step 2. Otherwise, return to the program menu (use option 9) to select another program or exit from QSB (use option 0).

Example

To demonstrate the use of MKV, consider the following example problem. Market surveys conclude that if a customer buys brand A product now, then he will have a .2 probability of buying brand A product again, a .3 probability of buying brand B product, and a .5 probability of buying brand C product. Similarly, if he buys brand B or C, he will have different probabilities of buying different brands next time. Table 16.1 shows these transition probabilities. Jimmy is the average customer and he

CHAPTER 16

bought brand B this time. What is the probability that he will buy brand A the next two times? What are the probabilities that Jimmy will buy brand A, B, or C in the long run?

Table 16.1. Transition probabilities

This time	Next time	A	B	C
A		.2	.3	.5
B		.4	.3	.3
C		.2	.4	.4

Step 1. Analyze the problem and prepare the initial probability vector and transition probability matrix.

Initial probability vector: < 0 1 0 >
Transition probability matrix:
    A B C
A .2 .3 .5
B .4 .3 .3
C .2 .4 .4

Step 2. Enter the data (the data underlined in the following figures will be entered into QSB):

2.1. Enter problem name MARKET.

2.2. Enter the information shown in Fig. 16.2 to define the problem. Note the conventions that appear on the screen when you enter data.

```
                    MKV Data Entry for MARKET

Please observe the following conventions when entering a problem:

(1) Respond to the questions that seek general information about a problem.
(2) Then enter the names of states unless using defaults.
(3) Then enter the initial state probability vector, if known.
(4) Then enter the transition probability matrix.
(5) After you enter your data, press the ENTER key.
(6) On the same screen page, you may correct errors by pressing
    the BACKSPACE key to move the cursor to the required position.
(7) When you are satisfied with the data on a page, press the SPACE BAR.
(8) When entering a problem, press the Esc key to go to a previous page;
    press the / key to go to the next page.

How many states are there in your problem? (Enter number ≤ 50 )      <3 >

Do you know the initial state probability vector (Y/N) ?             <y >

Do you want to use the default names of states (S1,...,Sn) (Y/N)?    <n >
```

FIGURE 16.2. Screen display of MKV for defining a problem.

2.3. Figure 16.3 displays the screen for defining the names of states. Note that you could use default names (S1, S2, and S3). After entering the names, press the SPACE BAR.

```
          Enter the Names of States using at most 6 characters
        (To use default names, i.e., S1, . . ., Sn, press the ENTER key)
States:
     1: <A    >  2: <B    >  3: <C    >
```

FIGURE 16.3. Screen display for defining state names.

2.4. Figure 16.4 displays the screen for entering the initial state probabilities, which are $< 0\ 1\ 0 >$.

```
           Enter the Initial State Probability Vector for MARKET

A:      0_____    B:     1_____    C:      0_____
```

FIGURE 16.4. Screen display for entering initial state probabilities.

2.5. Figure 16.5 displays the screen for entering the transition probability matrix.

```
           Enter the Transition Probability Matrix for MARKET Pg 1
From    To
A       A:     .2____   B:   .3____  C:   .5____
B       A:     .4____   B:   .3____  C:   .3____
C       A:     .2____   B:   .4____  C:   .4____
```

FIGURE 16.5. Screen display for entering transition probability matrix.

Step 3. You may display or print the entered data, as shown in Fig. 16.6.

```
   Input Data Describing Your Problem MARKET (Initial State Probabilities)

A:      0.0000   B:     1.0000   C:     0.0000

     Input Data Describing Your Problem MARKET (Transition Probability Matrix) Pg 1
From    To
A       A:     0.2000 B:    0.3000 C:    0.5000
B       A:     0.4000 B:    0.3000 C:    0.3000
C       A:     0.2000 B:    0.4000 C:    0.4000
```

FIGURE 16.6. Screen display of the MKV data.

CHAPTER 16

Step 4. You have the option of modifying the data as needed. This gives the menu displayed in Fig. 16.7.

```
              Option Menu for Modifying MARKET
    Option
       1   ----   Modify the initial probability vector
       2   ----   Modify the transition probability matrix
       3   ----   Add one state
       4   ----   Delete one state
       5   ----   Display and/or print input data
       6   ----   Return to the function menu
```

FIGURE 16.7. Option menu for modifying an MKV problem.

Step 5. You are now ready to perform the Markov process. Select option 5 from the function menu. This will call up the solution menu displayed in Fig. 16.8. Note that if you select option 1 from the solution menu, you will see every iteration on the screen. These iterations are illustrated in Figs. 16.9 to 16.13. You also can specify the number of iterations for the process by selecting option 3 from the solution menu.

```
                 Option Menu for Solving MARKET
    When solving a problem, you can display every iteration of the
 Markov process.  You may specify the number of iterations (≤ 32000);
 otherwise, the program continues iterations until approximate steady
 state is found.  Steady state is attained as the differences of prob-
 abilities of the same state between consecutive periods are ≤ 1.0E-6.

    Option
       1   ----   Solve and display each iteration
       2   ----   Solve and display the final iteration
       3   ----   Solve without displaying any iteration
       4   ----   Specify the maximum number of iterations
       5   ----   Return to the function menu
```

FIGURE 16.8. Option menu for performing the Markov process.

```
              Initial State Probabilities -- Iteration 0

  A:     0.0000    B:     1.0000    C:     0.0000
```

FIGURE 16.9. Iteration 0—initial state.

```
                  State Probabilities -- Iteration 1
A:      0.4000   B:      0.3000   C:     0.3000
```
FIGURE 16.10. Iteration 1—one period later.

```
                  State Probabilities -- Iteration 2
A:      0.2600   B:      0.3300   C:     0.4100
```
FIGURE 16.11. Iteration 2—two periods later.

```
                  State Probabilities -- Iteration 3
A:      0.2660   B:      0.3410   C:     0.3930
```
FIGURE 16.12. Iteration 3—three periods later.

```
              Final Iteration -- Total Iterations = 9
A:      0.2679   B:      0.3393   C:     0.3929
```
FIGURE 16.13. Final iteration—steady state.

Step 6. After the Markov process iterations are finished, you may use option 8 in the function menu to display or print the final state probabilities. The menu of options available for displaying or printing is shown in Fig. 16.14. If you choose option 2 from this menu, the final state probabilities and recurrent period for each state are displayed and automatically printed, as shown in Fig. 16.15.

```
Option Menu for Displaying and/or Printing the Final Solution to MARKET
       You have the following options available for displaying
       or printing the final solution.  If you want to print the
       solution, make sure that the printer is ready.

       Option

             1   ----   Display the final solution only
             2   ----   Display and print the final solution
             3   ----   Return to the function menu
```
FIGURE 16.14. Option menu for displaying and printing MKC results.

```
              Final Iteration -- Total Iterations = 9
A:      0.2679   B:      0.3393   C:     0.3929
                 Recurrent Period for Each State
A:      3.73     B:      2.95     C:     2.55
```
FIGURE 16.15. Final results for the market problem.

CHAPTER 16

Step 7. By choosing option 6 from the function menu, you can save the problem on a data disk(ette). Make sure that your data disk(ette) is formatted and inserted in the disk(ette) drive. Figure 16.16 gives the screen display for saving a problem.

```
          Decide on a file name for saving your problem.
          The file name may be the same as the problem name.
          Type x:xxxxxxxx.xxx for your file name ( e.g., A:XYZ.DAT ).

What is your file name (Type A:, B:, or C: to see all the files) ? a:MARKET.dat
```

FIGURE 16.16. Screen display for saving a problem.

Exercises

1. A laboratory has conducted an experiment about the random walk of an animal. From some preliminary tests, if the animal goes to the right this time, the probabilities that it will go to the right, left, up, or down next time are .2, .4, .4, and 0, respectively. The table summarizes these probabilities. What is your prediction concerning how many times the animal will turn to the right or left in 100 walks? Assume the animal's first turn is right.

Transition probability matrix

	Right	Left	Up	Down
Right	.2	.4	.4	0
Left	.1	.3	.4	.2
Up	.7	.1	.1	.1
Down	.2	.3	.1	.4

2. Consider the system with the following initial probability vector and transition probability matrix.

Initial probability vector:
   < .1 .2 .3 .05 .05 .1 .05 .15 0 >

Transition probability matrix:

	s1	s2	s3	s4	s5	s6	s7	s8	s9
s1	.1	.05	.1	.2	.05	.3	.1	.1	0
s2	.05	.05	.1	.15	.15	.1	.2	.1	.1
s3	.15	.15	.05	.05	.15	.2	.05	.1	.1
s4	.2	.3	.05	.15	0	0	0	.1	.2
s5	.1	.2	.05	.05	.15	.2	.05	0	.2
s6	0	.3	.1	.2	.1	.1	.05	.15	0
s7	.5	.1	.05	.05	.05	.1	0	0	.15
s8	.2	.1	.05	.15	.15	.15	0	.1	.1
s9	.1	0	.2	.1	.15	.1	.05	.2	.1

a. What is the probability s5 occurs at the fifth period?
b. What is the probability s3 occurs at the tenth period?
c. What are the probabilities of each state in the long run?

3. In a certain state a voter is allowed to change his party affiliation (for primary elections) only by abstaining from voting in the primary for at least one year. Let D, R, A respectively indicate that a person votes Democratic, votes Republican, or abstains from primary voting in any given year.

a. If the following one-step transition probability matrix represents general voting behavior in the state, what is the probability that a person abstaining this year will abstain 2 years from now?

	D	R	A
D	1/2	0	1/2
R	0	3/4	1/4
A	1/2	1/2	0

b. Last year one half of the population voted Democratic, 1/4 Republican, and the remainder abstained. What do you expect to be the voting proportions in the next primary given the above transition matrix?

c. In the long run, what proportion of the population will be voting Democratic, Republican or abstaining in the primary elections? Again, assume one-step transition matrix given above.

Chapter 17
TIME SERIES FORECASTING (TSFC)

Overview of the TSFC Decision Support System

This program allows you to perform time series forecasting using the following popular methods: simple average, moving average with constant process, moving average with linear trend process, single and double exponential smoothing, adaptive exponential smoothing, and linear regression. TSFC requires time series data that may be entered from keyboard or from files on a disk(ette). Up to 50 historical data are allowed for forecasting future trends. However, up to 20 observations can be displayed on the screen or printed if you choose to plot the results. TSFC can make forecasts for up to 17 periods into the future. These can be displayed on the screen or printed. Also, when each forecasting process is complete, the program will display the mean absolute deviation (MAD), mean square deviation (MSD), and bias for each process.

TSFC allows you to use up to three forecasting models simultaneously and to plot or display the results on the screen. By pressing the F8 key, you may print the output on the screen at any time.

Special Notes on the TSFC Program

1. When entering a problem, use the BACKSPACE key to move the cursor to the position where you want to make corrections.

2. The TSFC program will calculate up to a 15-period forecast based on the historical data. TSFC also provides different methods, which have been described above, to compute the future forecasts. Some of the methods require users to enter additional parameters. For example, the moving average requires the number of moving periods, and the exponential smoothing requires smoothing constant and/or trend constant.

3. You have the option to plot the forecasts on the screen.

4 The plot of the future forecast ranges from the minimum historical data to one and a half times the maximum historical data.

Solving Problems with TSFC

When you first select TSFC, the function menu, shown in Fig. 17.1, will appear. You can now select the appropriate option. The steps for using TSFC to solve a forecasting problem are listed below:

Time Series Forecasting

```
Welcome to your Time Series Forecasting (TSFC) Decision Support System!
         The options available for TSFC are as follows.
  If you are a first-time user, you might benefit from option 1.

     Option              Function

       1      ----    Overview of TSFC Decision Support System
       2      ----    Enter new problem
       3      ----    Read existing problem from disk(ette)
       4      ----    Display and/or print input data
       5      ----    Perform forecasting
       6      ----    Save problem on disk(ette)
       7      ----    Modify problem
       8      ----    Display and/or print final solution
       9      ----    Return to the program menu
       0      ----    Exit from QSB
```

FIGURE 17.1. Function menu of the TSFC program.

1. Prepare the historical data and appropriate parameters.

2. Enter the problem into QSB (use option 2) or read the existing problem from a data disk(ette) (use option 3).

3. Display or print the problem if you want to check and verify data (use option 4).

4. Modify the problem as necessary (use option 7).

5. Perform forecasting (use option 5).

6. Display and print the final solution (use option 8).

7. Save the problem on a data disk(ette) if you may need it again (use option 6).

8. If you want to solve other problems, go to step 3. Otherwise, return to the program menu (use option 9) to select another program or exit from QSB (use option 0).

Example

To demonstrate the use of TSFC, consider the following example. The sales volume of a company for the last 15 months is shown in Table 17.1. By using the five-month moving average, double exponential smoothing with smoothing constant 0.6 and trend constant 0.1, and linear regression, forecast sales for the next five months.

CHAPTER 17

Table 17.1. Sales volume for the last 15 months

Month	Sales volume	Month	Sales volume
1	398	9	430
2	395	10	460
3	290	11	465
4	400	12	473
5	410	13	480
6	425	14	465
7	450	15	485
8	440		

Step 1. Prepare the historical data and model parameters, as shown in Table 17.1.

Step 2. Enter the problem (the data underlined in the following figures will be entered into TSFC):

2.1. Enter problem name and number of historical data (observations) as shown in Fig. 17.2.

```
Please name your problem using up to 6 characters ? SALES
Your TSFC program can accept up to 50 historical observations.
How many observations are there in SALES ? 15
```

FIGURE 17.2. Screen display for entering problem name and number of data.

2.2. Fig. 17.3 displays the screen for entering historical data.

```
                    TSFC Data Entry for SALES

    Period  Observation     Period  Observation     Period  Observation

      1      <398 >           6      <425 >          11      <465 >
      2      <395 >           7      <450 >          12      <473 >
      3      <290 >           8      <440 >          13      <480 >
      4      <400 >           9      <430 >          14      <465 >
      5      <410 >          10      <460 >          15      <485 >
```

FIGURE 17.3. Screen display for entering observations.

Step 3. You may display or print the data as shown in Fig. 17.4.

Time Series Forecasting

```
              Input Data Describing Your Problem SALES
 Period   Observation         Period   Observation        Period   Observation
    1      <398    >             6      <425    >           11      <465    >
    2      <395    >             7      <450    >           12      <473    >
    3      <290    >             8      <440    >           13      <480    >
    4      <400    >             9      <430    >           14      <465    >
    5      <410    >            10      <460    >           15      <485    >
```

FIGURE 17.4. Screen display of observations.

Step 4. You have the option of modifying the data as needed. This gives the menu displayed in Fig. 17.5.

```
            Option Menu for Modifying SALES
     Option
        1    ----    Modify observation
        2    ----    Add one observation
        3    ----    Delete one observation
        4    ----    Display and/or print input data
        5    ----    Return to the function menu
```

FIGURE 17.5. Option menu for modifying a TSFC problem.

Step 5. You are now ready to solve the problem. Select option 5 from the function menu. This will call up the forecasting menu displayed in Fig. 17.6. Note that you may choose up to three models at one time to perform forecasting. If you use arrow keys to choose options 2, 5, and 7 and select option 8 to perform the forecasting, the forecasting process is as shown in Fig. 17.7.

```
            Option Menu to Perform Forecasting for SALES
       You have the following options for making your time series
   forecasting.  You may choose up to 3 forecasting models and then
   use option 8 to run the models.  The program will ask you for the
   appropriate parameters for the selected models.  After performing
   forecasting, return to the function menu to display the results.
     Option
        1    ----    Simple average (AV)
        2    ----    Moving average (MA) -- Constant process
        3    ----    Moving average (LT) -- Linear trend process
        4    ----    Single exponential smoothing (SE)
        5    ----    Exponential smoothing with trend adjustment (ET)
        6    ----    Adaptive exponential smoothing (AE)
        7    ----    Linear regression (LR)
        8    ----    Perform forecasting
        9    ----    Return to the function menu
```

FIGURE 17.6. Option menu for performing forecasting.

CHAPTER 17

```
For how many periods into the future do you want to forecast (≤ 15) ? 5
Moving average (MA) with constant process starts.
What is the moving period (up to the number of observations) ? 5
MAD =   28.56   MSE =   1152.944              Bias = -28.56
Exponential smoothing with trend (ET) adjustment starts.
What is the smoothing constant ( α ) ( < 1.0) ? .6
What is the trend constant ( β ) ( usually between 0.1 and 0.3) ? .1
MAD =   27.42469          MSE =   1519.504       Bias = -8.453903
Linear regression (LR) starts.
MAD =   20.9899           MSE =   860.7222       Bias = -6.801084
Slope =  8.878571         Intercept =  360.0382
Forecasting complete.
```

FIGURE 17.7. Process of forecasting.

Step 6. After the forecasting is performed, you may use option 8 in the function menu to display or print the final results. The menu of options available for displaying or printing is shown in Fig. 17.8. If you choose option 6 from this menu, the final results from the three selected forecasting models are displayed, plotted, and automatically printed, as shown in Figs. 17.9 and 17.10.

```
Option Menu for Displaying and Printing the Final Results to SALES
        You have the following options for displaying or printing the
forecasting results.  If you want to print the results, make sure
the printer is ready.

        Options
            1   ----  Display the final results only
            2   ----  Display and print the final results
            3   ----  Plot the final results
            4   ----  Plot and print the final results
            5   ----  Display and plot the final results
            6   ----  Options 2 and 4
            7   ----  Return to the function menu
```

FIGURE 17.8. Option menu for displaying and printing TSFC solution.

Results of forecasting			
Observation	MA	ET	LR
1 398	16 473.6	487.1317	502.0953
2 395	17 473.6	492.2887	510.9739
3 290	18 473.6	497.4457	519.8525
4 400	19 473.6	502.6026	528.7311
5 410	20 473.6	507.7596	537.6096
6 425			
7 450			
8 440			
9 430			
10 460			
11 465			
12 473			
13 480			
14 465			
15 485			

FIGURE 17.9. Results of forecasting.

Time Series Forecasting

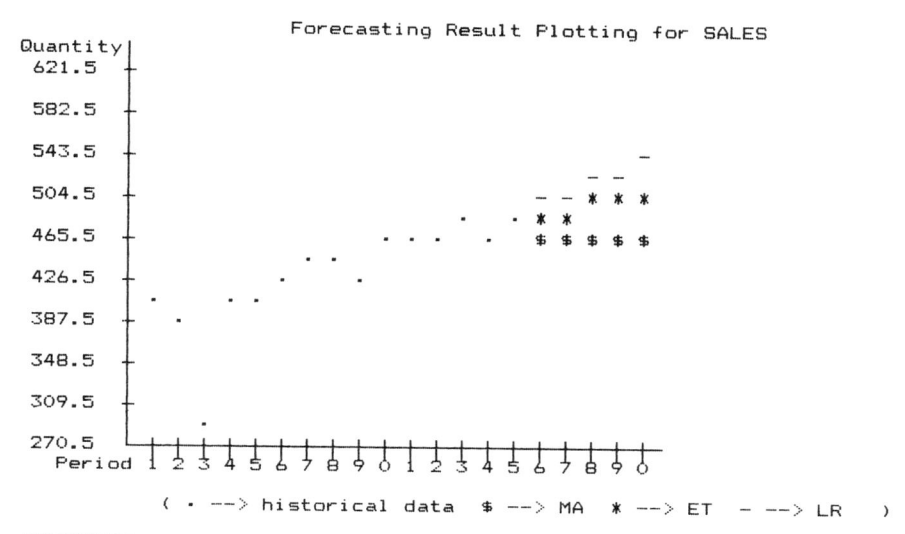

```
Quantity|     Forecasting Result Plotting for SALES
  621.5 +
  582.5 +
  543.5 +                                    - -
  504.5 +                              - - * * *
                                  . . * *
  465.5 +                    . . .     $ $ $ $ $
  426.5 +              . . .
  387.5 +         . .
  348.5 +
  309.5 +
  270.5 +   .
        +--+-+-+-+-+-+-+-+-+-+-+-+-+-+-+-+-+-+-+-+-
  Period  1 2 3 4 5 6 7 8 9 0 1 2 3 4 5 6 7 8 9 0

        ( . --> historical data   $ --> MA   * --> ET   - --> LR )
```

FIGURE 17.10. Plot of the results of forecasting.

Step 7. By choosing option 6 from the function menu, you can save the problem on a data disk(ette). Make sure that your data disk(ette) is formatted and inserted in the disk(ette) drive. Figure 17.11 gives the screen display for saving the problem.

```
              Decide on a file name for saving your problem.
           The file name may be the same as the problem name.
        Type x:xxxxxxxx.xxx for your file name ( e.g., A:XYZ.DAT ).
  What is your file name (Type A:, B:, or C: to see all the files) ? a:SALES.dat
```

FIGURE 17.11. Screen display for saving a problem.

Exercises

1. Forecast the sales volume for the next three years. The last ten year sales volumes are listed below:

Year	Sales
1	48123
2	47560
3	48535
4	49638
5	50135
6	51136
7	52470
8	51636
9	52798
10	53001

a. Use the linear regression to perform the forecasting.
b. Use the adaptive exponential smoothing with alpha = .3 to perform the forecasting.
c. Use the three-year moving average to perform the forecasting.
d. Compare the performance for the above methods.

2. For the following historical data, forecast the next five-period sales by using the following methods:
a. Three year moving average
b. Three year moving average with trend
c. Exponential smoothing with alpha = .5
d. Compare the performance for the above method

Period	Sales
1	$390150
2	430253
3	390158
4	380139
5	385125
6	380125
7	378652
8	373439
9	356215
10	312059
11	336025
12	311038

3. Repeat problem 2 by using the following data:

Period	Historical data
1	415
2	386
3	435
4	535
5	437
6	398
7	365
8	421
9	374
10	395
11	411
12	432
13	405
14	379
15	397

APPENDIX—SELECTED EXERCISE SOLUTIONS

Chapter 4

1. a. X1 = 35.1351, X2 = 35.9459, OBJ = 712.4324
   b. C1: 4.8 to 14.6667, C2: 6.5455 to 20, B1: 129.0909 to 394.4445, B2: 450 to 1375
2. a. A = 150, B = 0, C = 240, OBJ = -809.9999 (-810)
   b. 11, 4, and 0
3. X1 = 0, X2 = 104.5789, X3 = 0, X4 = 75.7632, X5 = 0, X6 = 19.6579, OBJ = 1813.921
4. X = 276.9231, Y = 54.6154, Z = 70, OBJ = 6716.154
5. Clerks for shifts 1 to 6 are 9, 2, 10, 5, 0, 1, respectively. Total clerks = 27.
6. AR (grade A to regular) = 37500, BR = 0, CR = 12500, AH = 35000, BH = 0, CH = 35000, AS = 0, BS = 0, CS = 40000

Chapter 5

1. X1 = 35, X2 = 36, OBJ = 712
2. X1 = 0, X2 = 104, X3 = 0, X4 = 76, X5 = 0, X6 = 20, OBJ = 1812
3. X1 = 1, X2 = 3, OBJ = 5
4. a. X1 = 1, X2 = 1, X3 = 1, X4 = 0, X5 = 1, OBJ = 115
   b. X1 = 1, X2 = 1, X3 = 1, X4 = 1, X5 = 0, OBJ = 103
5. Xc(Coal) = 1100, Xn = 0, Xh = 400, OBJ = 597
6. a, b: X1 = 0, X2aVendor II, price 1) = 0, X2b = 300, X3a = 0, X3b = 100, OBJ = 19650
7. X11 = 1, X13 = 1, X22 = 1, X24 = 1, Y1 = 1, Y2 = 1, Obj = 130.
8. a. X11 = 500, X22 = 500, P1 = P2 = 1, A = B = 1.
   b. The same as a.
9. T1 = 80, T2 = 78, O1 = O2 = 0, N1 = N2 = 0, P1 = 332, P2 = 468, Inv = 32.

Chapter 6

6. 1R1 (Month 1, Regular production for month 1 demand) = 1000, 2R2 = 1000,
   2O2 (Month 2, Overtime production for month 2 demand) = 200, 3R3 = 1000,
   3O3 = 500, 4R4 = 1000, 4O4 = 800, 5R4 = 200, 5R5 = 800, 5O5 = 800,
   6R6 = 1000, 6O5 = 200, 6O6 = 500, OBJ = 102800

Chapter 7
6. Child 1: F D, 2: C G, 3: E, 4: B, 5: A, OBJ = 47.4

Chapter 8
6. Link 1-2, 1-3, 2-4, 3-6, 3-7, 7-5, OBJ = 9600

Chapter 9
3. CP: A-D-G-J, Tcp = 13
4. a. CP: 1-2-5, Tcp = 11, Total cost = 24000 + (2500)(3)
   b. Crash: 1-4 one day, 2-5 two days, Tcp = 9, Total cost = 26500 + 2500
5. b. CP: A-E-H-K, Tcp = 26, Total cost = 45300 + 1500
   c. Crash: E one week, Tcp = 25, Total cost = 45500, CP: A-E-H-K and C-F-H-K

Chapter 10
5. a. CP: A2-A6-A8-A10, Tcp = 12
   b. 2.28 percent
   c. Decision: renegotiate, expected cost = 700
6. a. CP: D-H-J, Tcp = 15
   b. .1933
   c. Decision: extend, expected cost = 325
   d. 17 days

Chapter 11
1. 1-2-5-9-13-16, OBJ = 50
2. 1-2-5-9-14-18-21-23-25, OBJ = 91
3. Display items 4, 5, 8, and 9, total return = 24
4. Buy stock 1: 4 thousands, 2: 4 thousands, 3: 2 thousands, total return = 15 thousands
5. Production schedule: 8, 14, 13, 13, 0, 8, total cost = 18610
6. Production schedule: 0, 2, 6, 6, 6, 7, 0, 6, 4, 2, total cost = 12240

Chapter 12
4. a. EOQ = 707.1072, inventory cost = 282.842
   c. Order 1000, total cost = 15250
5. a. Order 985
   b. Order 1128

Chapter 13

3. No
4. Cost for clerk = 5 + 1.33(4) = 10.333
   Cost for machine = 7 + 0.66(4) = 9.64
   Decision: machine

Chapter 14

5. a. Lq = 0.3, W = 14.92 seconds

Chapter 15

5. a. A (no survey)
   b. $52.98
6. a. Buy the second
   b. Buy the second - test by friend

Chapter 16

1. R: .3103, L: .2759, U: .2759, D: .1379
2. a. S5: .1036
   b. S3: .0857
   c. .1321, .1448, .0857, .1332, .1036, .1370, .0635, .1001, .0999